THE KINGDOM OF KIND

Written by Jenny Phillips

Cover design by Phillip Colhouer

Illustrations by Kessler Garrity
Colored by Nada Serafimovic

goodandbeautiful.com

TABLE OF
CONTENTS

Introduction

Read to the child: I'm excited to read this book with you. I'll read the sections following the parent/teacher banner. You'll read the sections following the student banner. I'll help you with difficult words.

Reading this book together increases your enjoyment of reading and your reading speed, accuracy, and confidence. It will also help you practice decoding difficult words and increase your vocabulary, which is all the words you know the meanings of.

Before reading each chapter, we will complete a practice page. In many chapters I will read vocabulary words, their definitions, and example sentences that use the words. Each vocabulary word will then be used in the chapter.

Most words from the Challenging Words List break English phonics rules (often because they originated in a foreign language). You will most likely need to learn the challenging words by sight rather than sounding them out. Thus, all the challenging words (listed on the next page) will be repeated in multiple lessons.

Eric Nathan Peter Rose Milo Dune

Challenging Words List

These words—which are difficult to decode (sound out) phonetically—are included repeatedly on the practice pages.

conquer	machine	silhouette
coupon	meringue	spaghetti
crepes	omelet	suite
croissant	pistachio	theory
dungeon	rhinoceros	

Vocabulary Words

These words are learned on the practice pages, included in the chapters, and reviewed in the *Level 3 Course Book*.

aghast	elaborate	loathsome
broad	evade	meager
chasm	initial	shrouded
dumbfounded	intrigued	

Practice Page Principles

Level 3 Phonics Principles

These principles are reviewed repeatedly on the practice pages.

- CH can say /k/ or /sh/
- Decoding skills
- GUE can say /g/
- IE can make the long E and long I sound
- INE can say /in/ or /een/
- Long and short vowels
- ON, ION, and EON can say /en/, /un/, or /yen/
- Phonograms review
- TU can say /ch/
- TURE can say /chur/
- Y in the middle of a word

PHONICS

Decoding

Many children can read difficult words by guessing the word in the context of a sentence. It's helpful to gain and practice the skill of decoding words. Then children can avoid guessing or skipping difficult or unfamiliar words. By design, these practice pages include unfamiliar words (like "boilerplates") at times, forcing the child to sound out the words. You needn't look up or explain the words' meanings, as they are used as phonics exercises and not helpful vocabulary words. Read to the child: **A phonogram is a letter or group of letters that together make a single sound. The green boxes in this course show phonograms that almost always say the same sound.**

1. Say the sound of the phonogram in green.

2. For each purple box, say the sound of each circled phonogram, and then read the word. If needed, sound out the parts of the word as given below the word.

oi

oil

b(oi)l(er)p l a t e s
boi ler plates

oa

oat

l(oa)d m a s t e r
load mas ter

VOCABULARY

Read the vocabulary section to the child. The vocabulary words given on practice pages are included in the chapter and throughout the book.

Initial means happening first or at the beginning.

My initial reaction when I saw a snake was to freeze.

Chapter 1: The Gold Coins

If you use your imagination, you might be able to picture the Kingdom of Kind with its vast forests, turquoise lakes, and rolling hills of rich soil and long, waving grass. Knights, peasants, merchants, and royalty dwell in the valleys and hills. Just behind the kingdom loom towering gray mountains with their craggy peaks often veiled in mist.

One chilly autumn evening, when daylight was fading and night was descending upon the kingdom, Prince Eric, the king's only son, was riding back to the castle. His carriage suddenly swerved around a corner as the drivers tried to avoid a stretch of thick, oozing mud. Much to the prince's disappointment, the carriage came to an abrupt halt. One of the wheels sank deep into the moist, mushy mud.

"Ugh!" cried the prince to his drivers with a hint of impatience. "Hurry up already, and get me out of here! I am getting cold, and I'm not safe here."

PARENT/TEACHER

The prince stuck his head out the window and sighed as his men took out coils of rope and went to work trying to free the carriage.

"Come on, hurry, hurry! I have a dinner appointment with the king at seven o'clock," the prince complained.

A slight motion just beyond the mud patch caught the prince's attention. An old, feeble woman wearing a worn, patched dress and a ragged shawl came hobbling in the direction of the carriage and looked directly at the prince.

"Please, Your Highness," she entreated with a gentle, humble voice, "have you any food?"

With emotion in her voice, she briefly told the prince of her sad plight. Her husband and two children had died years ago, and her fingers had become old and stiff. She could no longer weave or sew to earn a living. That very day she had been cast out of her home because she had no money to pay the rent for her dilapidated cottage. She was traveling to a relative's home many miles away but had no way to obtain food or shelter until she arrived.

The prince took her story into consideration. Initially, he was suspicious of the old woman, and he was most definitely upset by this disruption.

Surely she has brought these conditions upon herself by not planning ahead and saving her money, the prince rationalized in his mind. *I cannot help every poor peasant. The castle would be overrun with beggars.*

The prince sighed heavily. He didn't like looking at the woman, with her ragged clothes and sorrowful face. He just wanted her to go away.

He thought of the leather pouch full of gold coins resting on his thigh. There was no question that even one coin would delight the old woman and feed her for an entire week.

It would not be a disappointment to lose just one coin, thought the prince.

He fished a single coin out of his pouch. With a feeling of satisfaction, he leaned out the window and threw the shiny coin, aiming for the woman's feet just beyond the mud. But as he did so, seven gold coins spilled out of the pouch and quickly sank out of sight into the oozing mud.

Bothered, the prince shook his head. *This wretched situation has spoiled my evening*, he thought miserably.

He had no intention of getting dirty by searching for the coins, nor did he want to be delayed any further by having his drivers search for the lost money.

Just then the drivers jumped back onto the carriage. "It is all taken care of, Your Highness," one said. "We will have you back to the castle in twenty minutes."

As the carriage started to roll, the prince motioned to the old woman, who was wrapping her worn shawl tightly around her cold shoulders. "If you can find the coins," said the prince, "they are yours to keep."

As the carriage drove on, the prince snuggled back into his warm velvet seat. His initial reaction was to be extremely annoyed that he had lost the precious coins. But upon further reflection, he decided that the woman would most likely find the coins. *Yes, she might have to get a little muddy,* thought the prince, *but she is sure to find the coins. Then she will be fed for nearly two months.*

Feeling quite satisfied with himself, the prince wrapped up in a warm blanket. A proud expression crept across his face. *Yes*, he thought, *I was mighty generous tonight.*

But then the prince shook his head. *Surely she didn't need eight coins. She may not even live long enough to need them. Even one coin would have shown great compassion.*

Nevertheless, within minutes he had forgotten all about the old woman's plight and was thinking of the delicious broiled lamb steaks, warm gingerbread, and luscious custard he would soon be eating by bright candlelight in the warm, spacious castle.

Not long after the prince left, another poor peasant, a man named Drogo, came to that same patch of mud, shivering as he pulled his cart of tools. When he veered to the right to avoid the oozy ground, his expression changed to confusion. The daylight was nearly gone, but he could still make out the shape of an old woman kneeling and digging in the mud.

Chapter 2: Practice Page

Parent/teacher note: As learned in *Timothy of the 10th Floor*, syllable division rules are complex (even for adults) and inconsistent. Also, reading words broken into syllables is not always the easiest way to read words. Thus, in this program, children learn how to decode longer, more challenging words by looking for known phonograms and breaking the words into smaller parts, which don't need to be at syllable breaks.

🔊 **PHONICS**

Decoding

Read to the child: **Say the sound of each phonogram in the green boxes.** Hints are below each box if needed.

gn	oa	oi	er	kn	ai
g̲naw	o̲at	o̲il	he̲r	k̲not	rai̲n

Point to each phonogram with a circle around it, say the sound of the phonogram, and then read the whole word.

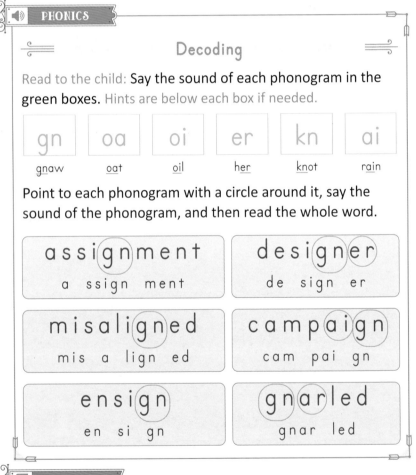

ass i(gn)ment

a   ssign   ment

desi(gn)(er)

de   sign   er

misal(ign)ed

mis   a   lign   ed

camp(ai)(gn)

cam   pai   gn

ensi(gn)

en   si   gn

(gn)(ar)led

gnar   led

🔤 **VOCABULARY**

Read the following information to the child:

Meager means too small in amount.

His meager supplies ran out.

Chapter 2: Drogo

PARENT/TEACHER

Drogo was at first frightened by the haggard figure kneeling in the mud. Then he was saddened. Darkness was dropping down on the vast valley, and the temperature was becoming colder by the minute. The old woman had to be freezing! He feared she wasn't thinking clearly and was in danger out on the road all alone.

But he rationalized to himself, *I cannot do anything to help this woman. I myself am poor and must get home to my wife before it gets too dark. Someone will come along and help her. Perhaps her family is already looking for her.*

"Please go home," he called gently, but firmly.

The old woman looked up. "I have no home anymore." She pointed to the mud. "I am searching for gold coins that fell into the mud," she said with desperation.

Drogo shook his head, thinking the poor woman was indeed crazy. As he hurried on toward home, thoughts of the woman would not leave him.

When he walked through his doorway, the merry sound of the crackling fire and the sweet smell of corn cakes greeted him. He kissed his wife, Hazel, and explained the situation to her. As he gave a description of the poor woman's meager clothing and unusual actions, his wife's eyes filled with tears.

"I can't leave her there alone to stay outdoors in the cold. The poor woman said she had no home," Drogo said. "I have a strong impression that I should go back and help her."

"That is the right decision," replied Hazel with emotion. She hugged him tightly. "Hurry! I will start on the preparations for our special guest."

Drogo ran along the dirt road with his now empty cart bumping behind him. It began to drizzle, and the moisture snuffed out the lantern Drogo was using to light the road. Blessedly, as the humble peasant pressed on, the rain stopped, and the skies began to clear. Then Drogo used the stars in the vast sky, the glowing moonlight, and the occasional flash of distant lightning to find his way.

Although he wished he had decided to help the woman when he first saw her, all he could do now was hurry back to find her.

At last, breathing hard, he reached the location where he had last seen the old woman, but she was no longer by the mud. Disappointment flooded his heart.

Just then a slight noise made him swing his head to the left side of the road. There he found the old woman curled up under a bush, trembling with cold. She had not been able to find any of the coins that had sunk into the mud.

"Hello. My name is Drogo," he said. "I came back to invite you to join my wife and me for supper and offer you a warm, safe place to sleep."

🌿 **PARENT/TEACHER**

The woman was so cold and weary that she could give only an appreciative nod and a weak smile.

The strong man lifted her gently into his cart. She was muddy and wet from the rain, so he took off his coat and wrapped it around her.

They met no other travelers on the road. The silence of the night was broken only by the hoot of an owl, an occasional breeze moving through the trees, and the creak of the wooden cart wheels.

Finally, they reached Drogo's small wooden cottage. To the woman, the cottage was anything but humble—it seemed like a palace! Bright, cheerful flames danced in the fireplace; the savory smell of boiled potatoes and steamed cabbage filled the air; and a soft pattering echoed from the roof as the rain started again.

Hazel motioned to the old woman. "Come, sit by the fire. My name is Hazel."

"Thank you. I am Mabel," she answered, easing onto a stool by the fire. She wept softly at the kindness of these strangers and rejoiced in the warm shelter and food.

Drogo and his wife laid straw bed mats out by the fire, giving up their bed for Mabel to sleep on. Hazel held out her nightgown, insisting that Mabel change out of her wet dress.

As soon as Mabel's head hit the pillow, she was asleep. For the first time in a long time, she slept in warmth with a glowing peace in her heart.

It was late the next morning when Mabel finally awoke, and bright sunlight was pouring through the little wood-framed windows. Drogo and Hazel had been moving around as quietly as mice so as not to wake her, knowing she could use the extra sleep after her difficult experience of being stranded by the roadside last night.

Hazel had washed Mabel's dress and dried it by the fire. "Come!" said Hazel to the old woman. "Eat breakfast while you tell us your story."

Mabel's eyes became misty as she looked in gratitude at the golden square of butter floating on her steaming mush before starting her story.

After Mabel finished her breakfast, Hazel combed out her gnarled hair and put cream on her rough hands.

An hour later, Mabel was sitting in Drogo's cart. "Oh, I'm really not sure I can let you pull me all the way to my relative's home," she said.

"Nonsense," said Drogo cheerfully. "It's no trouble at all. You shouldn't be walking all that way in this cold."

Hazel handed a small basket to Mabel. "Drogo's as strong as an ox. Don't worry. Here, please take this bread and cheese and a jug of pear juice to enjoy along the way."

Hazel waved as the cart rattled off.

Peace and joy filled the hearts of Drogo and Hazel that day, and God rejoiced over their compassion toward a needy woman.

STUDENT

The actions of the prince and the majority of the people in the kingdom were not like Drogo's and Hazel's actions— not at all. Kindhearted people were quite rare in the land. There was constant contention in the kingdom, and selfishness lived in the hearts of many people. Bickering and mean gossiping abounded. Only a few families in the kingdom could actually be considered nice.

So, you might ask, why was this land called the Kingdom of Kind? Well, no one in the kingdom was sure, but they would eventually find out.

Chapter 3: Practice Page

Parent/teacher note: As the child reads aloud, help him or her slow down and sound out challenging words by pointing out known phonograms and dividing words into smaller parts.

PHONICS

Y in the Middle of a Word

Read to the child: **Y can make the short I sound (as in SIT) in the middle of a word. Read the words on the chart.**

gym	lyric	hymn
mystery	myth	oxygen

Read to the child: **Y can make the long I sound (as in LINE) in the middle of a word. Read the words on the chart.**

rhyme	python	cycle
analyze	style	recycle

Review from *Timothy of the 10th Floor*. Read to the child: **AR can make the sound /air/ as in CARRY. Read the words on the chart.**

comparison	transparent	barrel
secretary	narrate	revolutionary

VOCABULARY

Read the following information to the child:

Broad means wide.

The broad porch had plenty of room.

Chapter 3: On the Castle Balcony

Do you remember the prince who threw a coin at the old woman's feet? Let me tell you more about this twenty-one-year-old young man. His name is Prince Eric. His story is an important piece of the puzzle that will tell us why his kingdom was named Kind.

Was Prince Eric kind? No, he was not. He was so self-centered that he was scarcely aware of any person around him.

For instance, he had never given any thought to who prepared the superb meals delivered three times a day on fancy dishes or who took care of the acres of splendid gardens around the castle. He had never once thanked his father, the king of Kind, for anything. He had never even been required to do any work! He had servants to do all the work for him.

He was very smart when it came to manipulating people and getting his way, but he was not very wise. In fact, he knew very little about the world around him. A young man named Nathan was assigned to do all the prince's reading and studying so the prince could be free to ride his horse, take naps, and go hunting.

Perhaps this is why Prince Eric felt so generous when he tossed the poor old woman a coin. If I were to write a story about another time he gave something to someone, it would go like this: "Once upon a time, there was a prince who never gave anything to anyone. The end."

A week after Drogo helped the peasant woman, Prince Eric sat on a castle balcony. The sunset was painting the sky a vivid yellow hue and laying patterns of light across the vast lawns surrounding the castle.

But Prince Eric didn't see nature's artwork; he was hiding from his servant Nathan, who liked to give him a daily report of his work. At a marble table, the prince sat counting gold coins. He loved the clinking sounds they made as he stacked them.

"Ah, Prince Eric!" Nathan called as he strode onto the balcony. "There you are. I've come to give a report."

Prince Eric gave a disappointed grunt.

"Today," Nathan began with a broad smile, "I wrote the lyrics for two new hymns, memorized an entire page of poetry, and learned twenty new French words for you. I hope Your Highness is pleased with what you learned today."

Prince Eric looked up with a scowl. "Well, I think it is a shame I am learning only one foreign language. I should learn Italian, too. People will think I am smarter if I learn Italian. Start tomorrow."

Nathan was thrilled! "Yes, Your Highness!" he replied in a jolly voice. "Thank you very much."

The prince was annoyed. "You act as if you actually enjoy learning and studying. It bothers me. Stop it this instant! I am giving you more duties and more work. Why would you thank me for that?"

"Sir, I truly like studying," said Nathan, unable to conceal his broad smile.

"Why?" the prince inquired.

"Because it makes me happy."

The prince held up a gold coin. "How many gold coins do you have?"

"Two, sir."

The prince laughed. "Two? You have two gold coins, and you think you are happy. I have five hundred thousand gold coins, three hundred rubies, and eight hundred diamonds."

"And yet," said Nathan, "you are not happy."

The prince stood up abruptly. "What did you say?"

Nathan gulped, and his eyes grew big and round as he realized he had made a grave mistake.

"Of course I am happy!" cried the prince. "How dare you tell a lie. Go away to your home, wherever that may be, and never come back to the castle. Never!"

Half an hour later, the mountains were fringed with the last light of the sinking sun. A few stars twinkled in the sky. Prince Eric leaned against the balcony railing and watched Nathan, a lone figure, walking away down the castle drive. *Hmmmph. Good riddance,* thought Prince Eric, ignoring a terrible pang of loneliness swirling inside him.

Then he leaned forward and peered intently into the dusky night. *Why has Nathan stopped?* thought Prince Eric.

STUDENT

Nathan had stepped off the road and was fumbling in his bag as he looked around. He then stooped down by a tree and was obviously doing something.

How strange! thought Prince Eric. *Is he digging? Is he carving something on the tree?* The prince was bursting with curiosity.

"What are you doing?" Prince Eric called, but his voice was drowned out by the swift river that ran under the castle and cascaded down a cliff between three arches at the castle's base.

"I must know what he is doing!" the prince declared aloud. "I'll go see for myself."

He turned, flipped his red cape behind him, and strutted across the balcony. The soldiers guarding the front castle entrance started following him, as he was never supposed to leave the castle unattended.

"Don't follow me!" yelled the prince. "I am just going out on the castle grounds."

Obediently, the soldiers returned to their posts as Prince Eric hurried away. When he reached the spot where Nathan had been, Nathan was nowhere in sight.

PARENT/TEACHER

"Rats!" said Prince Eric. With a big huff of annoyance, he stepped off the road and looked around. *What was Nathan doing?* he thought. *What tree was he by? I'm not sure, but I know he was doing something, and I must know what it was!*

The last glow of sunlight had melted into the dark, craggy mountains. Prince Eric shivered as he listened to the sound of crickets chirping and the lonely wind moving through the trees; he was not used to being alone outside at night. Another wave of annoyance washed over him as long sheets of gray clouds covered the light of the moon, making it too dark to continue his search.

STUDENT

A rattling sound made Prince Eric jump. From around the corner came a peasant man pulling his cart, the wooden wheels bumping on the cobblestones. A large lantern hung on a pole at the front of the cart.

"Stop!" demanded Prince Eric. "What are you doing here?"

The man, who happened to be Drogo, responded, "I just sold a batch of my goat cheese to the castle kitchen."

Prince Eric frowned as he walked around to look in the back of the cart. "Give me your lantern at once!"

Drogo hurried and took down the lantern. Prince Eric grabbed for it, and as he did, it fell into the layer of hay lining the cart. The whole cart burst into flames.

PHONICS

CH Can Say /k/

Read to the child: **CH can say /k/. Read the words. Use the hints or words broken into chunks as needed.**

chorus	chord	orchid
architect ar chi tect	**technical** tech ni cal	**scholar** AR can say /er/
ache Silent E makes A say its long sound	**technology** G is soft before E, I, or Y	**echo** A single vowel at the end of a word is often long

Challenging Words

Read the words repeatedly until you can read them all without help. These words can be memorized by sight as they are phonics rule breakers or very difficult to decode.

conquer

crepes

theory   croissant

dungeon

omelet   pistachio

silhouette

Chapter 4: Nathan's Note

PARENT/TEACHER

"Look what you have done!" cried Prince Eric as Drogo stepped back from the cart, coughing.

"Give me your cape!" Drogo cried. "I'll smother the fire."

"You've lost your mind!" shouted Prince Eric, clutching his cape. "Who would dare to ask a prince for his cape?"

Wind breathed into the fire, intensifying the flames that soon licked the side of the wagon and spread hungrily to the wheels. Drogo watched helplessly.

A minute later, Prince Eric felt a drop of rain on his head and then another on his shoulder. That was the only warning the gray clouds gave before releasing their heavy load. Rain began to fall in torrents, dousing the flames that engulfed the cart. Then as quickly as the rain had begun, it stopped.

Prince Eric moved away from the smoky, steamy, sizzling cart as Drogo frantically searched the ashes, trying not to burn himself. He pulled out a little cloth pouch that hadn't been burned and hugged it to himself with a heavy sigh of relief.

"What's in the pouch?" Prince Eric asked as he brushed his wet hair off his forehead, furious that he was soaked.

"Coins," said Drogo.

"Let me see," demanded Prince Eric, holding out his hand.

With a frown, Drogo handed over the pouch and watched as Prince Eric dumped its contents into his palm.

"Seven gold coins and a silver coin! Where did you get this money? Surely this is not from selling goat cheese."

Drogo hesitated before he spoke. "Only the silver coin is from selling goat cheese. The other gold coins came as a generous gift from you."

"What?" cried Prince Eric.

"The gold coins you threw in the mud. The old woman told me about them. You told her she could keep the coins if she found them. Then she told me that I could keep them if I found them. She . . . she didn't want anything to do with the coins. I searched for an entire day in the dried mud, and I found them."

"Obviously, these coins are mine." Prince Eric put all the coins in his pocket and tossed the pouch back to Drogo. "And I'll keep the silver coin as well—to cover the stress you have caused me and the time it will take my servants to dispose of your ruined cart."

"But . . ." Drogo stood in shock, with his mouth hanging open in disbelief. He turned to his half-burned cart, which still smoldered. As if on cue, a wheel broke off and rolled down the road.

Drogo hung his head and plodded down the hill to the dark valley, leaving his ruined cart behind.

Prince Eric, wet, angry, and fatigued, stormed up the hill to the towering castle.

The next day, Prince Eric did not awaken until lunchtime. The first thing he did after dressing was return to the area beside the road where he had seen Nathan acting suspiciously. In the bright sunlight, Prince Eric quickly found a note nailed to the base of the tree. It was slightly damp, but the thick tree branches had protected it from the rain. He ripped the note off the tree in excitement but then remembered he couldn't read. Grumbling, he folded the paper and stuffed it in his pocket. When he returned to the castle, he shoved it in his desk drawer and forgot about it.

Prince Eric walked around for days in a dark mood, not willing to admit that he missed Nathan. The king hired a cranky old scholar to take Nathan's place studying and learning for the prince.

But Nathan's words would not leave the prince: "And yet, you are not happy."

The prince began to realize that, indeed, he was not happy.

"I have the same routine all the time," the prince thought. "That is why I am not happy."

For years the prince had requested rolls and grapefruit for breakfast every morning. The rolls at the castle were soft and buttery—they practically melted in his mouth. And the grapefruits in the kingdom were the sweetest, juiciest grapefruits in all the world.

"No more rolls and grapefruit for breakfast," the prince ordered. "I want variety! New things!"

For three weeks he was served something different every morning: crispy bacon, tasty biscuits and gravy, silky cheese fondue, warm apple streusel, vegetable omelets, strawberry crepes, herb sausages, fluffy blueberry muffins, cinnamon toast, soft-boiled eggs, funnel cakes, fresh orange juice, peaches and cream, golden croissants, Italian doughnuts dipped in chocolate sauce, baked apples with walnuts and maple syrup, square waffles with whipped cream, hash browns and corned beef, and ham with a pineapple-mustard glaze.

But alas, the prince was no happier than before. And when the baker had expended all of her ideas and could think of nothing new to make him for breakfast, the prince ordered that she be cast out of the castle.

Then the prince decided he was bored—intolerably, insufferably bored. *Boredom must be the cause of my unhappiness,* he thought. He demanded that his servants bring him the best entertainment to be found.

Jesters juggled and told riddles. Skilled musicians played the harp and flute beautifully. Singers sang as smoothly and sweetly as nightingales. The bards dramatically recited poetry and long, eloquent speeches in honor of the prince.

The prince enjoyed the entertainment, but every time it ended, his unhappiness was still there with him, like a dark cloak covering the sunshine. He had nightmares of seven gold coins sinking endlessly in oozing mud. He refused to ask the scholar to read the note Nathan left, worried about what it might say. At times his heart opened up a sliver—just enough to shout, "YOU started the man's cart on fire. YOU took his hard-earned money!"

He decided he needed more thrilling entertainment to conquer his unhappiness. His servants brought in dancing polar bears from the Arctic, emperor penguins from Antarctica, fire swallowers and snake charmers from far-off lands, rhinoceroses that played with balls, and actors with fancy costumes and stage scenery.

His theory didn't work. He was still dissatisfied.

Finally, he took Nathan's note out of his drawer and brought it to his cranky scholar. He listened to the words as his scholar read it slowly.

> Prince Eric, your selfishness is a terrible prison. I will pray every day that you might find the way to free yourself.
>
> ~Your friend always, Nathan

Chapter 5: Practice Page

Parent/teacher note: If a child struggles with a word on the practice page or in the chapter, have the child first look for any known phonograms in the word and say the sound of the phonogram. If needed, tell the child the sound of the phonogram. Always try letting the child work with the word before helping, but help before he or she gets overwhelmed, or when you know it's a new principle for the child.

🔊 **PHONICS**

GUE Can Say /g/

Read to the child: **GUE can say /g/. Read the words in the boxes.** The G sound in TONGUE is formed more lightly.

plague	tongue	morgue
dialogue	league	epilogue

Challenging Words

Read the words repeatedly until you can read them all without help.

croissant	dungeon	crepes	omelet
conquer	pistachio	silhouette	theory

📖 **VOCABULARY**

Read the following information to the child:

Evade means to avoid.

Elaborate [ee–LAB–er–uht] means detailed or complex.
We like simplicity, so we try to evade elaborate plans.

Chapter 5: The Voyage

Nathan's note had confused Prince Eric. Thinking of the note filled him with anger. Then the next moment, the word "friend" danced in front of him but felt like a beam of disappearing sunlight he could never grasp. In the end he tore up the note and tossed it in the fireplace.

Prince Eric decided he'd stay so busy that he wouldn't have time to reflect upon his unhappiness, so he tried to evade his feelings by throwing himself into huge, important projects. He had statues created of himself, a spacious golden tower built to hold his jewels, and a new wardrobe made of elaborate clothes.

But still, the prince was utterly unhappy. His gloom only seemed to increase.

One evening he stared out his window. The night shadows deepened as moonlight streamed around the castle. *I've tried everything*, he thought to himself. *Happiness is not here. I know now that I must leave and find happiness elsewhere.*

The prince announced his intentions to take a voyage around the world in search of happiness. He left the next week with one hundred of his knights. Prince Eric stood on the deck of his ship as the huge white sails were unfurled and filled with wind. A salty breeze fanned through his hair, and the endless blue ocean lay before him. *Ah, at last,* thought Prince Eric, *I am headed to happiness. I must be. I'll search the corners of the earth until I find it.*

For an entire year, he searched the vast world. He ate exotic fruits and gourmet foods, met powerful kings, stayed in luxurious palaces, and bought rare jewels. He swam with sea turtles, bathed in splendid hot springs, and climbed the highest mountains. But still he could not find happiness anywhere.

He was plagued by the images of coins sinking into the oozing mud and a peasant's cart burning. And every now and then, the word "friend" swirled around him, but it vanished each time he reached out to take hold of it.

His sailors displeased him in different ways, and one by one, he dismissed them at different stops along the way until he had a crew of only seven men left to sail his ship. The men were scared of the prince. Even though they obeyed his commands, they steered clear of him.

"Nonsense!" Prince Eric declared to the wall of his ship's cabin one day as he lay on his velvet couch. "This search for happiness is nonsense."

The wall didn't speak back. It only creaked a little.

"I'm talking to a wall," Prince Eric said. "That's just the problem! I have no friends. I shall sail back home as quickly as I can, and I will hire twenty friends to visit me every day. They shall receive one gold coin every month, and they shall adore me and laugh with me and listen to my stories."

Prince Eric nodded to the wall. "See! I have solved the problem. At last I shall find happiness."

That very night, a storm arose on the ocean. It beat upon the ship's windows, it thrashed the ship's sails, and it whirled the ship across the water. Prince Eric stayed in his cabin. *My men will take care of things*, he thought.

Soon, Prince Eric realized that the crashing sound he was hearing was not thunder—it was the crashing of wood. The ship was starting to break up, and water was beginning to flow into the prince's cabin. He flew out his cabin door and looked around for his crew. Slanting torrents of rain and deep darkness made it hard to see. When a series of lightning strikes lit up the scene, Prince Eric spotted his crew on the lifeboat, rowing quickly away from the ship. "Hey, I'm the prince!" he called. "You must come back and get me!" But it was no use. Prince Eric knew his men had abandoned him.

Prince Eric held on to the railing as the ship tilted dangerously. Then a huge wave tore away his grip and sent him into the swelling waves. Shocked by the cold water, Prince Eric panicked. Another huge wave crashed upon him and then another. Just when he thought he couldn't keep his head above water any longer, he felt something bump into him. A small barrel! He wrapped his arms around it.

Eventually, the squall subsided, and the ocean grew calm. Eric shivered as he looked around. Moonlight reflected on an endless ocean that looked dark and eerie. All he wanted was to go to sleep in a nice, soft bed, but he couldn't close his eyes and risk drifting off to sleep.

The next day, he was even more tired. The sun blazed down on him, and he was painfully thirsty.

Finally, at the end of that day, just as the sun was setting, the prince was washed ashore on a little island.

Exhausted, thirsty, and starving, the prince crawled to a stream of fresh water and drank. His strength was gone, and he fell into a deep sleep on the grassy bank.

Chapter 6: Practice Page

CH Can Say /k/

Read to the child: **CH can say /k/. Read the words.**

chemical	chemist	chrome
chem ic al	chem ist	ch rome

scheme	technical	orchestra
sch eme	tech ni cal	or ches tra

CH Can Say /sh/

Read to the child: **CH can say /sh/. Read the words.**

chef	machine	Michelle
	INE can say /een/	

Challenging Words

Read the words repeatedly until you can read them all without help. This scene is from an upcoming chapter.

coupon

suite

meringue

machine

spaghetti

rhinoceros

Chapter 6: The Island

The afternoon sunlight danced on the prince's face, and the gentle breeze whispered in his ears. Instead of noticing how peaceful his surroundings were, he let anger and annoyance fill him. He drank from the clear stream again and then heard a noise—laughter. Looking around a bush, the prince saw a little girl, obviously a peasant, and her father.

The father sang a tune as his daughter smiled and giggled. Then the little girl picked wildflowers and danced and twirled in the streaming sunlight. Her father caught her up in his arms and hoisted her onto his shoulders, and they started on a path to the forest.

"Wait!" cried the prince.

The father turned in surprise as the prince weakly stumbled toward them. He was a pitiful sight with torn clothes, a dirt-smudged face, and messy hair.

"I am Prince Eric. I was shipwrecked, and I demand that you tell me where I am."

The man bowed slightly. "You are on a small island in your kingdom—the farthest island from the castle. And I fear you will be here for quite some time. No one on the island has a boat big enough to sail the great ocean. A ship comes once every three months with supplies. It just came two days ago, so it won't return for three months."

"Outrageous!" screamed the prince as he stomped his foot. "I cannot stay on this pitiful island."

"Is it pitiful?" asked the man with a kindly smile. "We rather love this place."

The prince narrowed his eyes as he studied the man. "You remind me of someone."

"Yes, I am sure I do," said the man. "I'm Peter. Perhaps if you come to our cottage with us, you will discover the reason why I remind you of someone. You are welcome to stay with us until the boat arrives in July."

"I absolutely will not stay in a cottage!" stated the prince as he stomped his foot.

"As you wish," replied the man, and he turned to leave.

The prince suddenly realized his plight. If he did not go with the man, where would he stay? What would he do?

"Fine!" called the prince. "I will come with you."

When they arrived at the cottage, the prince was hesitant to go through the doorway. He had never entered a cottage before, and he did not know what to expect. But as he stepped into the small one-room cottage, the aroma of freshly baked wheat bread surrounded him, gentle yellow sunlight poured in through the windows, and white curtains fluttered peacefully in the breeze. The man's wife sat on a rocking chair, cradling a pudgy baby with soft black curls.

"I feel odd," said the prince as he stepped farther into the cottage. "Very odd, indeed. I feel as if—"

But his words were stopped short by a cheery, familiar voice behind him.

"Hello, Father! Hello, Mother! I'm home!"

The prince turned and stood face-to-face with his former servant Nathan. Now the prince understood why Peter had seemed familiar—he was Nathan's father.

Nathan stood in astonishment.

The prince didn't know how to react. Here he was in dirty clothes, starving, and at the complete mercy of this family.

Peter quickly explained the situation, and Nathan closed his mouth, bowed to the prince, and said, "Prince Eric, you must be starving. Please have a seat, and we will serve you."

The prince was feeling even more odd. He sat silently as he ate, secretly savoring the warm bread and steaming oatmeal. As he observed the family, he became more and more amazed at what he saw. Here, in this tiny one-room cottage, he had found—happiness. Something deep inside him knew it and longed for a piece of it.

He stood up. "I demand you tell me how you found happiness. I have been to the corners of the earth in search of it, but it is here that I find it, and I insist that you give me the secret to happiness."

The room became instantly silent, and the children all left.

But Peter soon spoke up as a wise plan formed in his mind. "Your Highness, there are three keys to happiness, but I will share the keys with you only on one condition—you do exactly as I say for the rest of the time you are here."

"Absolutely not!" cried the prince. "I do whatever I want. No one tells me what to do."

"Then I shall not give the keys to you, Your Highness," said Peter.

"I shall throw you in prison when I return home," declared the prince.

"So be it," said Peter, beginning to clear the dishes.

For three days the prince demanded the keys to happiness. Peter held firm and would not share the keys unless the prince agreed to do whatever he asked.

The prince had no intention of taking orders from this man. But finally, after seeing how adamant Peter was, the prince gave in and agreed to the terms.

"We begin in the morning!" cried Peter happily.

As the family and the prince ate their porridge and cream the next morning, Peter asked the prince a question.

"Who cooked your food at the castle?"

"The cook."

"Yes, but who was the cook? What was her name?"

"I have no idea," said the prince. "I never stepped foot inside the kitchen. I never had any reason to meet her."

"I see," said Peter. "You never thanked her for the food?"

"Of course not," said the prince with annoyance in his voice. "Absolutely not! A prince is never required to thank a servant. A prince is never required to thank anyone."

As the dishes were being cleared, Peter asked gently, "Who cooked your meal today, Prince Eric?"

"Your wife, of course," replied Prince Eric.

"You could thank her."

"I will not."

"I insist," said Peter. "Remember our deal."

Prince Eric swallowed and squeaked out a tiny "Thank you."

Peter then took the prince to a meadow close to his cottage, laid out a blanket for the prince to sit on, and said, "I will return in two hours. When I return, I will ask you to tell me forty things you enjoyed observing—forty things you are grateful for in this field."

"Impossible!" objected the prince. "I will not."

"I'll be back in two hours," called Peter over his shoulder as he left. "If you do not have forty things, our deal is over."

PHONICS

Decoding + Long and Short Vowels

Read to the child: **Say the sound of each phonogram.**

aw	ur	igh	er	ai	gn
j<u>aw</u>	t<u>ur</u>n	h<u>igh</u>	h<u>er</u>	p<u>ai</u>d	<u>gn</u>aw

A vowel has a long and short sound. A long vowel says its name. When reading, if you are not sure if a vowel is long or short, try the short sound first. If that doesn't work, try the long sound. Point to each C, G, or GG in a purple word below and say its soft sound (if it comes before E, I, or Y) or its hard sound. Then read the whole word. If needed, sound out the word in parts first.

refrigerator
re fri ger a tor

OR can say /er/

amphibian
am phib ian

IAN can say /ee-in/

illustrator
ill u stra tor

photogenic
pho to gen ic

exaggerate
ex agg er ate

excellence
ex cell ence

certification
cer ti fi ca tion

centimeter
cent i me ter

Chapter 7: Fifty-One Things

The prince sat for an entire hour before he thought of the first thing to be grateful for. He had no idea what he was supposed to look for. What was he supposed to enjoy in a meadow outside a peasant's cottage? But the thought of never finding the keys he so desperately wanted made him try harder.

And then it happened.

A beautiful, bright-blue butterfly floated gently down onto a single white flower growing near the edge of the blanket. The prince was fascinated and hardly dared to breathe for fear of disturbing the butterfly and making it leave. The delicate wings, the vibrant color, the wonder of the tiny creature—the prince felt something stir inside him, but he hardly knew what it was.

"I like you, little fellow," the prince said. "I like watching you. You are first on my list."

After that it was not hard for the prince to come up with forty things that he enjoyed observing. In fact, he came up with fifty things for which he was grateful.

🌿 PARENT/TEACHER

Unable to wait for Peter to return, the prince ran wildly to the cottage, and he even let out a little *whoop* as the breeze pushed back his hair. "Yes, little breeze, I enjoy you, too! That is fifty-one things!"

He arrived at the cottage out of breath, and his words gushed out as Peter listened with utter pleasure.

"I enjoy eagles. I enjoy soft grass and sunshine. I enjoy little earthworms burrowing in the ground. I enjoy the smell of flowers. Oh, and I definitely enjoy clouds! I enjoy the sound of the stream, the song of the birds . . ." and his list went on.

"Well then," Peter said, "we should thank the One who created all those things." Peter bowed his head. "Go ahead, Eric."

"I will not—" the prince began, but then he changed his mind. "Will you show me how?" he asked quietly.

The next morning, Peter announced that Prince Eric was not going to eat any more bread until he took wheat from the fields and baked his own bread.

The prince held a stalk of wheat in his hand. "There is no way bread is made from this weed," he said.

Peter smiled. "You are going to need a lot more than just one stalk. Let's get started."

Prince Eric learned that day how to cut wheat, gather it in sheaves, and thresh it by beating it on a hard stone floor with a tool that removed the grain from the rest of the plant. He learned how to grind the wheat at a mill. He learned how to knead flour into a dough and make bread.

But he learned much more that day. He learned to enjoy his muscles working as he breathed in the fresh, sweet air and felt the warm sun on his skin. He learned to appreciate all the effort that went into baking a loaf of bread.

And as he finally took a bite of the warm bread he had made, feelings of satisfaction and contentment washed over him—feelings that came as a result of hard work.

There was goodness inside of Prince Eric that longed to surface and find life. The prince apologized to Nathan, and they became good friends. Under the gentle guidance of Peter and Nathan, the three keys to happiness were planted into the prince's heart: gratitude, service, and work. Over the next two and a half months, Eric learned to read, devoured all the books he could find, discovered a love of nature, drew close to God, and rejoiced in working.

One day, a storm swept over the island. The next morning Eric took a walk out to the sand dunes on the east side of the island. He enjoyed the soft, cool sand on his bare feet as he trekked across the rolling hills of sand. He finally reached the shoreline and slowly breathed in the salty, wet air. The only sounds around him were the faint cry of seabirds and the crash of the froth-capped waves hitting the sand.

On the far end of the beach, Eric noticed that the storm had washed up a bunch of wood planks from shipwrecks, something Peter had said happened often on that beach. Eric smiled as an unfamiliar but wonderful thought shot through him—the thought of doing something to serve someone else. Peter had taught him that the greatest and happiest leaders are those who don't focus on being served but on serving others.

I can gather this for wood for Peter and his wife to use in their fireplace once it dries out in the sun, Prince Eric thought as he ran down the beach.

After gathering a big bundle of wood together and tying it up with a long, thin piece of seaweed, he started back toward Peter's cottage. As he was passing some big clumps of tall beach grass swaying in the wind, he heard a sound that made him stop. It was whimpering.

A little set of brown furry ears poked out of the grass. Slowly, Eric put the wood down and parted the grass. His heart melted as he discovered the tiniest little puppy he had ever seen, shivering and looking up at him with big brown eyes.

"Hey, little guy," Eric said gently as he scooped up the trembling creature and nestled him in his coat. "Why are you out here all alone?"

This, too, was a new experience for Eric. He had never cared for an animal before, but he felt his heart bursting with love for the little ball of fur he carried.

The island was not big, so it didn't take long for Peter and Eric to find the puppy's owners and discover that it had wandered off during the storm. Eric was surprised to find out that the puppy was a tiny type of dog and wouldn't get much bigger. He was even more surprised when the owners told him that the sweet puppy was just old enough not to need its mother's milk and asked if Eric would like to have it.

Eric gratefully accepted the puppy and called him Dune because he found him in the sand dunes. The prince and the puppy became the best of friends as they explored the island's forests and beaches.

Chapter 8: Practice Page

🔊 **PHONICS**

ON, ION, and EON

Read to the child: **Read the words on the chart in which ON, ION, or EON says /en/, /un/, or /yen/ (in red).**

reason	carton	on**ion**
legion	napoleon	horizon
abandon	un**ion**	pigeon
region	luncheon	rebell**ion**

Challenging Words

Read the words repeatedly until you can read them all without help.

rhinoceros

coupon

machine

spaghetti

suite

meringue

📖 **VOCABULARY**

Read the following information to the child:

Dumbfounded means astonished or amazed.

When he told me that she found a chest of gold, I was dumbfounded.

Chapter 8: Milo

The three months passed much too quickly for Eric, who felt as if he would rather stay in Peter's humble cottage than return to the castle. But he was also eager to share the keys to happiness with the people of his kingdom. So he said farewell to the family and boarded the supply ship with Dune.

No one on the ship recognized Eric as the prince, and he decided not to tell anyone. He was disappointed by the other passengers, who were very different from Peter and his friends on the island. Grumbling and complaining were common on the ship.

"What a beautiful morning!" Prince Eric would say.

"It's cold and windy," the person would reply.

"What a lovely dinner!" Prince Eric would declare.

"The food is stale and dry," was the reply.

There was also a huge problem with stealing on the ship, and the passengers guarded their possessions closely. Mothers scolded their children harshly, and children pushed and shoved one another.

On the second morning of the voyage, Prince Eric saw a boy with freckles and sandy-blonde hair sitting alone on the deck, quietly staring out at the endless sea.

Taking a seat by the boy, Prince Eric asked, "What's your name?"

"Milo," came the hesitant, quiet reply.

"Why aren't you running around and playing?"

The boy frowned at Prince Eric. "I don't feel like playing," he mumbled before turning his head again toward the sea.

Prince Eric studied the boy. He looked so sad. His sandy-blonde hair was unkempt, and his clothes were ragged.

"Where are your parents, Milo? And why are you traveling on this ship?" Prince Eric asked.

The boy kept looking out at sea as he spoke. "I'm here alone. My parents sent me away on this ship. They can't feed me anymore, so I'm going to my aunt's house to live."

"Have you ever been to your aunt's house?" asked the prince. Milo shook his head.

"Well, maybe it will be wonderful living with your aunt!" suggested the prince.

"I'm sure it will be terrible," replied the sad boy.

Prince Eric sighed. "Why is it that so many people are negative? Don't you know that complaining and finding the bad in every situation make you unhappy?"

Milo shrugged his shoulders.

With another sigh, Prince Eric sat back in his chair and pondered. *How can I help this boy?*

After a few minutes, Prince Eric leaned forward in his chair. "Hey, would you like to play a game?"

Milo frowned. "A game? I don't think so."

"You don't even have to get off your stool to play this game," Prince Eric explained. "All you have to do is sit here and think of forty things you're grateful for."

Milo raised his eyebrows at Prince Eric. "Not only is that the weirdest game I've ever heard of, but it's also impossible. Forty things! I couldn't even think of one thing I'm grateful for."

"Ah, that is why you need the game so much," said the prince. "There's a reward for winning the game."

Milo sat up. "A reward? How much?"

"Oh, the reward is not money. But I'm not going to tell you what it is until you win the game. I'm going to leave. When I come back in thirty minutes, if you can tell me forty things you are grateful for, I'll give you the reward."

Prince Eric stood up. "I'll give you the first three items you can be grateful for. Do you feel the cool breeze on your face? You can be grateful for that. Do you see that big seabird sitting on the mast? You can be grateful you were able to see its beauty. Are you sitting on a stool? You can be grateful for that."

The boy looked dumbfounded as Eric walked away.

True to his word, Eric came back thirty minutes later. Apparently, Milo really wanted the reward and had worked hard to think of forty things he was grateful for.

"I thought of forty things! The boat hasn't sunk. I didn't bite my tongue during lunch. There were no bugs in my soup. I've never been struck by lightning. I haven't fallen off the ship and gotten eaten by a shark—"

Prince Eric listened with raised eyebrows to all forty things the boy said and then laughed. "Well, those weren't exactly the types of things I was thinking of, but I guess they are things for which to be grateful. For your reward I will let you play with my dog. His name is Dune."

"What!" cried the boy. He started protesting about what a terrible reward that was, but Prince Eric just reached into his big coat pocket and scooped up Dune. The adorable creature fit easily in one of Prince Eric's hands. Gently, he placed Dune on Milo's lap.

The boy stopped mid-sentence as Dune looked up at him and then licked his hand. A beautiful broad smile spread across Milo's face and seemed to crack away some of the hardness that had been there.

For the next few days, all Milo wanted to do was play with Dune. It made Prince Eric happy to see the boy smile and finally start running around the deck and playing. Dune seemed to adore Milo and always snuggled up in his lap. Prince Eric loved Dune, but he knew Milo needed him more than he did. So, when the ship arrived at Milo's stop, Prince Eric placed Dune into the boy's hands.

"He's yours if you want him," Prince Eric said, knowing that Dune made the boy feel loved.

"Oh! Yes! Yes! I want him," cried Milo.

Prince Eric watched Milo leave the ship and stand on the dock, looking around worriedly. No one seemed to be there for the boy.

The crew pulled up the ramp and untied the ropes, and the ship slowly started to sail away.

Still, Milo stood there on the dock, looking around. Everyone had hurried off, and only Milo and a few dock workers were left.

"Where is your aunt?" called the prince loudly from the ship's railing.

Milo turned around. Tears were streaming down his face as he shouted, "No one's here for me! I don't know what to do!"

Quickly, Prince Eric ran to the captain. "Stop the ship! I'm Prince Eric, and I demand you stop!"

The captain laughed. "I'm not stopping this ship for anyone, especially a man who thinks he's royalty."

In a flash Eric was back at the ship's railing. There stood Milo all alone, getting smaller and smaller. After stripping off his coat and shoes, Prince Eric climbed onto the railing, jumped, and managed to make a quite impressive, elegant dive into the cold, choppy ocean.

 **PHONICS**

Y in the Middle of a Word

Read to the child: **Y can make the short I sound (as in SIT) in the middle of a word. Read the words on the chart.**

gymnast	bicycle	crystal
cymbal	mythical	physical

Read to the child: **Y can make the long I sound (as in LINE) in the middle of a word. Read the words on the chart.**

rhyme	python	cycle
analyze	hydrogen	recycle

Review from *Timothy of the 10th Floor*. Read to the child: **When there is a double C followed by E, I, or Y, the first says its hard sound (/k/) and the second says its soft sound (/s/). Read the words. One word has two hard Cs.**

accepted	vaccine	accused
succeed	success	accented

VOCABULARY

Read the following information to the child:

Shrouded means covered.

The village was shrouded in fog.

Chapter 9: The Cave

PARENT/TEACHER

The coldness of the ocean water shocked Prince Eric. He fought his way to the surface of the ocean and then looked around to find the shore. He swam with powerful strokes, but his soaking wet clothes made it difficult. *I'm grateful for all the hard work Peter made me do on his farm*, thought Prince Eric, knowing he was in better shape than he used to be when he just lounged around the castle all day.

Milo had seen Prince Eric dive off the ship, and he was ready to greet him at the little rocky beach by the dock. Dune scampered over to where Prince Eric lay breathing heavily.

After a couple of minutes, Prince Eric regained his breath and stood up. "Milo, was your aunt supposed to meet you here?"

"Yes, my mom sent her a letter. Her husband died years ago. I don't even know where she lives on this island. I only know her name: Cassandra White."

Prince Eric shivered in his wet clothes and looked around at the deserted area. Even the dock workers had left now. Just up the road sat a little cottage with smoke curling out of its chimney.

"Come on," said Prince Eric, pointing to the cottage. "Let's get some help."

But help was not to be found at the cottage. The angry-looking woman who answered slammed the door on Prince Eric before he could say more than, "Can you help us? We . . ."

Prince Eric quickly realized that the island didn't seem very populated. There was only a small strip of rocky, flat land, and the rest of the island was covered in steep mountains. Currently, the tops of the mountains were shrouded in dark clouds. There were no other homes, shops, or buildings in sight. Prince Eric looked down at his bare feet and felt his wet clothes clinging to him.

Milo looked up at Prince Eric. "What should we be grateful for now?"

Prince Eric chuckled. "I'm not actually sure, Milo. Maybe it's just that you, Dune, and I are all safe and that we have each other. I guess we'd better follow this road and see what we can find."

For half an hour, they followed the road that cut up through the mountains. They saw no buildings or evidence of people. Prince Eric's bare feet were getting cut and bruised from the rocky road, so they stopped and found some really long ferns to wrap around them.

"Hey!" said Milo. "Are you grateful for fern shoes?"

"I sure am!" replied Prince Eric positively.

Just then they heard a rumbling noise.

A man came around the corner, driving a large wagon full of firewood. Prince Eric waved the man to a stop and explained their situation.

The man looked at Eric's fern shoes and his still-damp clothes and shook his head. "I can't help you. I have to get this firewood into my barn before the storm comes."

"What storm?" asked Prince Eric.

The man pointed to the east. Never before had Prince Eric seen such ominous black, swirling clouds. He shuddered, and the man started to drive away.

"Wait, let us come with you! Please help us!" cried Eric, but the man only urged his horses on faster, and the wagon rattled wildly down the road. A burlap sack fell from the back of the wagon, and Milo ran to grab it.

"Hey! This fell out!" he shouted as loudly as he could.

The man turned his head. "Keep it! I have no time!"

Milo hugged the bag to himself and ran back to Eric just as the first few drops of rain splattered to the ground.

"What are you grateful for now?" cried Milo over the wind, which had started gusting through trees near them.

Prince Eric looked around. "That cave!" he cried, pointing up to the mountain. "That looks like a cave opening. If we can get to it, we can have some shelter."

"The road doesn't lead to it!" said Milo.

"I know. We'll have to hike to it."

It wasn't long before the rain was coming down in slanting gray sheets. Soon after, darts of lightning and low, deep rumbles of thunder echoed throughout the mountains. The wind shrieked, and the hikers slipped time and again in the thick mud.

The cave entrance was up on a little steep ledge. Prince Eric let Milo climb up his back and shoulders to get onto the ledge. Milo was very careful not to hurt Dune, who was riding bravely in his coat pocket.

Then, using all his strength, Prince Eric tried to pull himself up onto the ledge, but he couldn't get a good enough grip on the wet, slippery rock.

Milo was a quick thinker. He took off his long coat, tied one sleeve tightly to the base of a bush, and dropped the other sleeve over the edge. Prince Eric grabbed the sleeve and, with a big burst of effort, got his elbows onto the ledge and pulled the rest of his body up.

Not knowing what they would find, but desperate to get out of the storm, they entered the cave. It went back only about ten feet, and then it turned and led to a narrow room. The room was dry and protected from the wind. Though the light was very dim, Prince Eric could see that there were no wild animals in the cave and breathed a sigh of relief.

Prince Eric and Milo sat down against the far wall, utterly exhausted.

"We did it," breathed Milo. "We made it."

"Thank you for helping me get up the edge, Milo. That was absolutely brilliant!"

Milo smiled broadly, and Dune licked his hand as if he were expressing his sincerest gratitude, too.

"I'm starving," said Milo after a few minutes.

"Let's see what's in the bag," suggested Prince Eric.

Carefully, Milo pulled out the contents of the wet bag. First, he pulled out a very large loaf of bread. It was smashed on one side and soggy on the other. Then he took out a leather pouch of what smelled like fresh apple juice. There was also a hunk of hard yellow cheese the size of an orange.

Dune didn't mind the soggy portion of the bread and gobbled it up. He also loved the piece of cheese Milo offered him.

The two friends listened to the roaring rain and shrieking wind outside the small cave as they ate the smashed, but dry, portion of the bread and the flavorful cheese. Though they shivered in their wet clothes, they were glad to be out of the weather. They both froze when they heard another sound very nearby at the cave entrance—a grunting sound and footsteps. Was it an animal? Was it a man?

Their questions were soon answered as the silhouette of a tall man in a long cloak suddenly appeared in the room.

Y in the Middle of a Word

Read to the child: **Y can make the short I sound (as in SIT) in the middle of a word. Read the words on the chart.**

gymnastics	lyrical	hymn
symbol	mythology	syrup

Read to the child: **Y can make the long I sound (as in LINE) in the middle of a word. Read the words on the chart.**

rhyme	python	tyrant
hyphen	typhoon	recycle

Challenging Words

Read the words repeatedly until you can read them all without help.

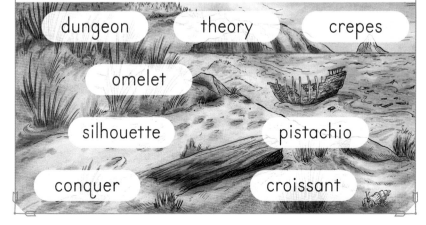

dungeon   theory   crepes

omelet

silhouette   pistachio

conquer   croissant

Chapter 10: The Mysterious Shepherd

In the dim light of the cave, Prince Eric couldn't tell if the man was a friend or a foe. He just stood there, dripping wet, staring at them. Finally he said, "Is there room here for a humble shepherd?"

The man's voice sounded very kind.

Prince Eric breathed a sigh of relief. "Yes, please come join us. I'm glad you also found some shelter from the storm."

The man gratefully sank against one wall and rummaged through his very large shoulder pack. Dune ambled over to sniff the man's leg.

"Cute dog you have there," said the man. "I've never seen one so small." He produced a lamp and matches, and within seconds a cheery light was dancing on the cave walls.

The shepherd studied Prince Eric and Milo. "I've never seen shoes like that either. Are those . . . ferns?"

Prince Eric laughed and then launched into the story of finding Milo on the ship and learning he was headed to his aunt's house. Milo dramatically told the part about Prince Eric diving off the ship, and then he told the shepherd how they ended up in the cave.

After listening to their stories, the shepherd rummaged in his bag again, taking out some random supplies. Prince Eric found himself gazing at the lantern. He didn't realize that he had let out a heavy sigh.

"What is wrong?" asked the shepherd.

"Oh—it's just a memory—of a lantern. There was a man, and I grabbed his lantern so forcefully that I set his cart on fire, and then I took some coins from him that I thought were mine. The memory pains me. I'm sure it was a great hardship for him to lose his cart. I long to find the man and repay him for the coins I took and the damage I did, but I don't know anything about him. I don't believe I will ever find him."

The shepherd studied Prince Eric. "You once were so unkind, but today you dove off a ship into the freezing ocean to help someone. You must be a changed man."

"I hope I am," replied Prince Eric humbly.

The shepherd then picked up some items next to him. He tossed Prince Eric a sturdy pair of leather moccasins and then a dry gray cloak.

"Oh, I couldn't possibly take these," Prince Eric replied, looking at the moccasins and cloak in amazement.

"You couldn't possibly *not* take them," replied the shepherd. "You'll never make it to Cassandra White's home with those fern shoes. She lives quite a distance from here."

"You know where she lives!" cried Milo.

"Yes, I passed by her home yesterday morning. She was the only person on this entire island who would even talk to me."

"I don't doubt it. Our kingdom has many unkind people, I'm afraid. But you, sir, are kind."

"I'm not from this kingdom," replied the shepherd.

"Oh, really?" asked Prince Eric curiously. "Where are you from?"

"A very faraway kingdom, actually. I came to deliver a message to the king, but I changed my mind when I saw him. I'm on my way back home now."

Prince Eric was shocked. "What made you change your mind about sharing the message with the king?"

"I've said enough," the shepherd replied. "I cannot talk about it, although I will say that my trip here has been disappointing. It's all been for nothing. I thought on my way back that I would at least visit the Great Cascade Waterfall on this island. It is supposed to be the highest waterfall anyone has discovered."

Prince Eric wasn't thinking of the waterfall. He wanted to know what message this shepherd might have had for the king, but the shepherd refused to say another word about it. Eric thought about telling the shepherd that he was the prince, but he decided it was best not to reveal his royal identity.

That night, Prince Eric was grateful for the dry cloak he had been given. But as he lay on the dirt floor of the cave, about to fall asleep, he saw Milo curled up in a ball and shaking with cold. Quietly, Prince Eric took off his cloak and wrapped it around the boy. Warmth filled Eric's heart.

It's funny, he thought to himself as he lay shivering, *how happy a person can be even while hungry and cold lying in the dirt.*

Hours later, Prince Eric opened his eyes, trying to remember where he was.

Milo woke up at the same time and sat up. "The shepherd is gone!" he cried. "But look, there's a note."

Prince Eric picked up the paper that the shepherd had left under a little stone. "It's a map to Cassandra's house. Let's get you there."

As they walked out into the warm sunshine, Prince Eric glanced back into the cave, wondering once again why a shepherd would have a message for a king.

Chapter 11: Practice Page

 **PHONICS**

CH Can Say /k/

Read to the child: CH can say /k/. Read the words in the boxes.

architect	chemistry	scheme
chemical	technical	stomach
orchid	orchestra	Christmas

GUE Can Say /g/

Read to the child: GUE can say /g/. Read the words in the boxes. The G sound in TONGUE is formed more lightly.

pla**gue**	ton**gue**	fati**gue**
dialo**gue**	lea**gue**	prolo**gue**

Review from *Timothy of the 10th Floor*. Read to the child: IOUS can make the sound /ē-us/ or /us/. CI can say /sh/. Read the words on the chart.

previously	precious	obviously
furiously	religious	spacious

Chapter 11: Homecoming

PARENT/TEACHER

After a day and a half of traveling, Prince Eric and Milo arrived at Cassandra's home, starving and exhausted. The little white home was perched on a hill in a long, narrow valley between two towering, steep mountains.

Cassandra had never received the letter Milo's mother had sent, but she was overjoyed to have Milo live with her. Her twins, a boy and a girl almost his age, heartily welcomed Milo to their home. Milo was excited to find out that Cassandra's family raised llamas. Blessedly, the family also had plenty of food and supplies to support Milo. Not only did they earn money from ropes they made with llama wool, but they also had a huge garden, goats, a healthy cow, and chickens.

Prince Eric knew he was leaving Milo and Dune in good hands, but it was still hard to leave them. However, he was more eager than ever to return to his palace. He had told Milo and Cassandra who he really was. Cassandra had told him that news had reached even her isolated home that the prince had died when his ship sank.

Because Cassandra's island exported many products, a supply ship stopped there weekly. Before long, Prince Eric was again on a ship headed home.

There was no grand homecoming for the prince. In fact, when he reached the castle gates, the guards called him an imposter and wouldn't let him in. He told them his entire story, but the guards only laughed. One guard said, "You? Prince Eric? In those ragged clothes and talking all sweetly? Be gone before we put you in the dungeon!"

Just then the king and his hunting party rode up to the gate. Despite Prince Eric's ragged clothes, the king recognized his son and was overjoyed to see him.

A banquet was thrown that night to celebrate the prince's return. He astonished everyone by thanking each servant. He even made his way to the kitchen, where he gave a hearty hug and thank you to the cook.

But that was nothing compared to what he did the next day: He insisted that he cook and serve breakfast to all the servants.

Even *that* didn't compare to what he did the next morning! Just as the sun was peeping over the hills and waking up the birds, the prince was seen out in the fields with the servants, plowing and sowing seeds and singing as he did so.

He thanked everyone all the time for everything: the gardeners, the stable boy, the tailor, the blacksmith, his father, and especially the Creator who made all the things he enjoyed. And he never failed to notice the brightness of the stars, the blueness of the sky, or the softness of a flower petal.

The prince never again bade anyone else to learn for him. In fact, he could not learn enough—he wanted to know about everything, and he devoured books as if they were chocolate cakes. He turned his golden tower into a library that was open to anyone in the kingdom. He traded in his luxurious wardrobe for a few outfits of simple, comfortable clothes to wear himself and five hundred well-made dresses that he personally gave out to all the widows in the kingdom.

"These things are simply not done!" cried his father with concern. "No prince does these things."

"You mean," said Prince Eric, "that no prince has ever done these things *before*. I am a prince. I do these things, and I love it!"

For the next several months, the prince taught his father about the keys to happiness. Together, father and son discovered endless exciting and beautiful doors that were opened by the keys of gratitude, service, and work.

Prince Eric invited Milo, Dune, and Cassandra and her family to visit the castle. Their visit brought the shepherd back to Prince Eric's mind. Excitedly, Prince Eric told his father about the shepherd and his undelivered message. Why would a shepherd travel from such a faraway kingdom to deliver a message to the king of Kind but then not deliver the message? They thought they might never know.

After his friends left, Prince Eric felt a little lonely again. He thought of Peter and his family and how happy he was there. Thinking about the love shared in that little cottage, a new thought formed in Prince Eric's mind: *I really want a wife and a family of my own.*

You might think the king planned a fancy ball to help the prince find a woman to marry. Actually, he threw seven fancy balls for the prince!

All the young ladies throughout the kingdom were invited.

At each ball, orchestras played, enormous vases of beautiful orchids lined the ballroom, and fruit punch, meringue pies, gingersnaps, and sugar-dusted sourdough doughnuts were served.

But the balls only left the prince fatigued. He could not find the kind of young lady he wanted to marry.

You see, almost all the people from the Kingdom of Kind were extremely selfish and thoughtless. The women had cruel tongues, gossiped constantly, and fought with one another. The men were rough and always scheming ways to cause their neighbors trouble. Men and women avoided hard work, and they let their houses and yards become untidy and run-down. The children were very naughty, too. They never said please or thank you. They punched each other's stomachs, coughed without covering their mouths, and said unkind things to one another. Even the pets were ill-behaved and continually nipped and growled and gnawed up all the furniture.

Prince Eric acknowledged that he had set a bad example for his kingdom for many, many years. Sadly, he knew it was going to be tough to change his kingdom, and his heart ached.

One morning, he sat in his room pondering as he looked out his castle tower window to the valley below. He believed he wouldn't find a wife who shared his values anywhere in the kingdom, so he would either have to look elsewhere or help his people change.

How long has the kingdom been like this? Prince Eric wondered. *And why was this kingdom named the Kingdom of Kind? Somehow I am going to find the answers to these questions!*

Prince Eric jumped up and strode out of his room. *I'm going to start my investigation right now!*

PHONICS

ON, ION, and EON

Read to the child: **Read the words on the chart in which ON, ION, or EON says /en/, /un/, or /yen/ (in red).**

religion	stallion	reunion
scorpion	onion	squadron
poison	luncheon	pigeon

CH Can Say /k/

Read to the child: **CH can say /k/. Read the words.**

architect	chameleon	anchor

Challenging Words

Read the words repeatedly until you can read them all without help.

machine	rhinoceros	suite
coupon	spaghetti	meringue

 **VOCABULARY**

Read the following information to the child:

Intrigued means to be fascinated.
 I studied the weird bug because it intrigued me.

Chapter 12: Ten Kings

Seated in the magnificent castle ballroom at three long banquet tables were the thirty oldest people in the kingdom. They had all been summoned to a luncheon at the castle.

After the meal was served, Prince Eric explained that he wanted to learn about all the past kings and everything any of them knew about the history of the kingdom. He questioned each one as they ate a twelve-course meal that was spread out over three hours.

Much to his disappointment, Prince Eric didn't learn anything that his father hadn't already told him. They all remembered stories about the last several kings, but none of them knew how the kingdom was founded.

Prince Eric then sought answers to his questions by reading all the history books he could find in the castle's magnificent library. What he learned intrigued him.

PARENT/TEACHER

Prince Eric's father was the tenth king of the kingdom. Eric read books about all the kings who had reigned—except for the first two. He couldn't find anything written about them.

One cold, foggy day, Prince Eric was in the library, searching once again for any information about the first two kings who had reigned in his land. Taking a break, the prince rubbed his tired eyes and then walked to the library window. Banks of heavy fog blanketed the valley, the tops of the tallest trees looking as if they were floating in the mist.

A servant's footsteps echoed in the vast stone library, and Eric turned to greet him.

"Christian! You have brought my lunch. How kind and thoughtful of you!"

Christian shook his head. Prince Eric had returned less than six months ago a changed young man. He was no longer vain and spoiled, but the servants were still not used to how thoughtful and kind Prince Eric had become. They especially were not used to being called by their names. No one had heard of a prince who bothered to find out a single servant's name, much less memorize the name of every servant in the castle!

"Your Highness," Christian said as he set the lunch tray on a table, "I am just doing my job. I was assigned to bring you lunch today."

"And you do such a superb job, Christian! Thank you for remembering to bring two lunches."

"You're welcome," replied Christian with an acknowledging bow of his head. "The cook said you always request two lunches."

"And that," said Prince Eric as he pulled out a chair and gestured toward it, "is because I want you to stay and eat with me if you would like. Please sit if you're hungry. The food smells delicious."

As they ate, Christian looked at the stack of books by Prince Eric. "What do you enjoy reading about?"

"Oh, everything. Last month I read many books about chameleons, orchestras, chemists, and even the life stories of an anchor maker and the architect of this castle! Every book was so interesting. But lately, I've been reading about the kings who reigned in this kingdom. Nothing was written about the first two kings. Have you ever heard anything about them?"

Christian shook his head. "No, never."

When Prince Eric bit into his roll, he frowned, set the roll down, and sighed.

"What is it?" inquired Christian.

"It's the roll. I appreciate the effort that went into making it, but it is a far cry from the rolls we used to have at the castle. In a fit of anger, I banished our amazing baker from the castle. She baked the most delicious rolls. They were buttery and flaky and practically melted in your mouth, and she had made them for me every morning since I was a little boy. I have had this kingdom searched high and low for the baker. Oh, how dearly I want to invite her—or rather implore her—to come back, but she cannot be found. She seems to have utterly vanished, and I have expended all my ideas to find her. No stone has been left unturned in our search, so I fear I must resign myself to a life without my treasured rolls."

Just then another servant appeared and bowed. "Your Highness, your father has fallen ill and requests your presence."

Prince Eric hurried to his father's sleeping chambers. He had been concerned about the king's health recently and now realized his father had become extremely sick and feeble.

"My dear son," the king said, "I am getting old, and I become fatigued easily. Now I am very ill; I may not live many more months. You have brought me so much joy. You have taught me the keys to happiness. Now I desire only one more thing before I die. You must marry. Not only do I desire to see you wed to a kind, lovely bride, but the law says the prince must be married in order to become king."

"Father, I want to be married more than anything. I cannot find a young woman anywhere with the character I am looking for, but I will continue to try."

Chapter 13: Practice Page

IE

Read to the child: IE can make the long E sound (as in MOVIE). Read the words on the chart. When you get to a word that is a dessert, tell me if you think it is tastier than a cupcake or not.

chief	thief	grief
belief	grieve	brownie
piece	niece	series

Read to the child: When the letters I and E together make one sound, like the long E sound, they make a phonogram. However, I and E are not always a phonogram when they are next to each other in a word. Read the words, in which I makes either the long I sound or the long E sound.

client	obedient	ingredient
cli ent	o be di ent	in gre di ent
orient	audience	nutrient
or i ent	au di ence	nu tri ent
fortieth	society	twentieth
for ti eth	so ci ety	twen ti eth

Chapter 13: The Baker's Daughter

Rose was the daughter of Tibby. And who was Tibby? Well, she was the baker who made the delicious rolls the prince missed so much—the same baker he banished from the castle.

After the prince threw Tibby out of her position as head baker of the castle, she moved as far away from Prince Eric as possible. Her years at the castle working for the selfish prince had been horrible. Also, she had been so disappointed in the people of the kingdom for their unkindness. Understandably, she no longer wanted to bake for the unkind, fussy people in the kingdom.

So Tibby and her husband, Nicholas, moved their family into a small cottage on a little island far away from any unkind people. In fact, Tibby, Nicholas, and Rose were the only people who lived on the island. There, near the shores of the mighty ocean, the happy little family started an orchid farm.

Rose had never lived in the castle. While her mother was a baker there, they had lived in a tiny, run-down cottage near the castle. Life had been very hard there. Now, Rose loved her life at the beautiful orchid farm. She loved her mother's scrumptious, home-cooked food and her thoughtful words. She loved her father's jolly character and his imaginative stories. Also, her father taught Rose to identify and appreciate all the plants, flowers, and trees in the area. She especially loved the orchids that her family grew. The exotic, colorful flowers filled the air with a sweet fragrance that mingled with the faint, salty smell of the ocean air.

Rose even loved the chores she was assigned, and she did them with a positive attitude. She loved the chorus of happy clucking from the chickens when she fed them. She loved hearing the pigs squeal with delight when she poured slop into their trough. She loved the smooth feel of dough as her mother taught her to knead and bake fabulous rolls.

Occasionally, though, Rose wished to meet people. She often longed for a friend, and she hoped to one day marry a caring young man. But there were two problems: their island was isolated, and there weren't many kind people in the kingdom anyway.

🌿 PARENT/TEACHER

One afternoon, after finishing her last chore, weeding the zucchini bed, Rose took a basket of bread and her favorite book and hiked up to the little grassy knoll above their cottage—a place she visited often. There she sat against the gnarled trunk of the huge old oak tree. She thoroughly enjoyed listening to the wind whisper through the trees like a thousand faintly tinkling bells.

Looking up into the tree, she thought, *I've never climbed this tree. Look! There's a perfect place to sit.*

Tucking the book in her pouch, she stood and started making her way up the tree. The sitting spot was not too far up, and Rose found it to be as wonderful a spot as she thought. After she sat there quietly for a few minutes, the birds dared come back to the tree, and Rose watched them in delight as they flitted around the branches.

Rose sang often, and she had a particular song that she loved. Her grandmother had taught it to her, and now she sang as sweetly as a nightingale from her perch up in the tree.

Oh, may my song echo across the ocean far
And reach to my Creator above the mighty stars.
He is the Grand Architect of all my eyes can see,
The Designer of the rolling hills and the chasms deep.
Oh, may my song echo across the ocean far
And reach to my Creator above the mighty stars.

After a few more minutes, Rose decided to climb down from the tree and get some bread from her basket. As she was going down through the branches, her leg struck the jagged edge of a small broken branch, leaving a long, deep cut on her shin.

Rose gasped in pain, and then she felt blood start to trickle down her leg. Hurriedly, she made her way down to her basket, grabbed the towel the bread was wrapped in, shook the crumbs from it, tore it into three long strips, and bound her wound. Wincing in pain, she stood up.

Just then, she spotted a familiar blue-and-white ship sailing toward their shore.

Quickly gathering her things, she made her way to the cottage, ignoring the pain in her leg.

"Mother! Father!" she cried. "Uncle Michael's ship is coming!"

Out of breath, Rose flew through the doorway of the little cottage and helped her parents hastily prepare for the guest who would soon be arriving. Michael, Rose's uncle, had planned to take Rose's father and loads of their orchids to the main city of the kingdom.

"Rose," said her father, "I've been having horrible stomachaches the last couple of days. I don't feel well enough to sail with Uncle Michael. Would you like to go in my place?"

Rose was delighted! She loved their little island, but she was ready for a new adventure.

Her throbbing leg, however, made her hesitate. *If Mother and Father know how bad this wound is, they won't let me go. I want to help Father and go on this trip. I won't say anything about my wound. After all, I'm an adult. I will nurse it myself and be very careful.*

She ignored her heart, which was trying to tell her that keeping her wound a secret wasn't the best choice.

Decoding

Read to the child: **Say the sound of each phonogram in the green boxes.** Hints are below each box if needed.

gn	oa	oi	wr	kn	dge
gnaw	oat	oil	wrap	knot	fudge

INE Can Say /in/ or /een/

Read to the child: **INE can say /in/. Read each word in the boxes.** As always, use the hints if needed.

determine	**famine**
de ter mine	fam ine

examine	**genuine**
ex am ine	gen u ine

imagine	**doctrine**
G is soft before E, I, or Y	doc trine

Read to the child: **INE can also say /een/. Read each word.**

wolverine	**submarine**
OL can say /ul/	A can say /uh/

tangerine	**nectarine**
G is soft before E, I, or Y	AR can say /er/

Chapter 14: The Children

As Rose traveled around the coast down to the capital city of the kingdom, she loved to stand on the deck and feel the salty breeze blowing through her hair. On the two-day voyage, her uncle told her a little about the prince's miraculous change of heart.

When they arrived in the city, Rose was excited to see the magnificent castle again.

"Is it true that the prince and the king have suddenly turned kind and generous?"

"Yes," Michael replied, "but I wish I could say that for the people of the kingdom. They still remain thoughtless and selfish."

Rose quickly saw that this was true. She was especially disappointed to see people shouting and laughing at a group of poorly dressed children sitting outside the castle walls. Some people even threw rotten fruit at them! Rose quickly ran over to shield the children.

"Children! Why do you stay here by the castle walls? Where are your parents?"

"We have no parents," said the oldest of the five children. "We are brothers and sisters. Our parents died of the plague four years ago. We have come from a faraway foreign land to the castle to beg help from the prince. We have heard of his kindness. But he is away until this evening, and we are waiting for him. The people do not want us here because we are poor and not from their kingdom."

"You sweet dears!" Rose cried. "How brave you are to have traveled so far. You must be so hungry."

Rose, once again ignoring the growing pain in her leg, retrieved her bag from the wagon. Her mother had packed a bag of her wonderful rolls. Rose distributed them to the children. Then, despite the children's dirtiness, she gathered them around her, setting the youngest in her lap. She taught them her favorite song, and then she told them all about the plants and flowers on her little island. She even told them some of her father's stories. As the children ate and sang and listened, their worries melted away, and for the first time in a long time, they felt peace and contentment.

Rose stayed with the children for a few hours, but then she couldn't wait any longer to go sell the orchids she had brought. Besides, she was starting to feel quite unwell. She hugged each of the children and told them to remember her song and sing it whenever they needed strength. The children noticed that she was limping heavily as she walked away.

When the prince arrived back at the castle that evening, the crickets were just starting to chirp. He was exhausted and hungry, but he heard that a group of orphaned children had come to petition his help, so he immediately went out the castle gates to meet the children. As he began to speak to them, he saw a couple of remaining rolls next to them. They were the exact shape and golden color of the rolls he had grown up eating.

"May I have a roll?" he asked the children.

"Of course!" they all said.

As the prince bit into the roll, he knew instantly that these rolls were made by the baker who once lived at the castle.

"Children! Who are you? Where did you get these rolls?" the prince cried.

As the children told the prince about their sad plight in life and the sweet and kind young lady who had so graciously given them the rolls, the prince's eyes widened, and his heart leaped.

"She sang to you and told you stories? And she had never met you before?"

"No, we had never met her before, but she spent hours with us, giving us encouragement and hope. She told us to sing this song whenever we needed strength," the oldest said.

The children then sang the song like a little choir:

Oh, may my song echo across the ocean far
And reach to my Creator above the mighty stars.
He is the Grand Architect of all my eyes can see,
The Designer of the rolling hills and the chasms deep.
Oh, may my song echo across the ocean far
And reach to my Creator above the mighty stars.

STUDENT

The prince could not believe it. "Children, I believe I have found my rolls and hopefully their maker, and I have been searching high and low for a young woman with this type of character to marry. Oh, but you must be so tired and hungry. Come into the castle. Let's get you some food and some baths and clean clothes. Then we shall sit around the fire while you tell me everything you know about this woman."

As they ate roasted nuts around the fire a couple of hours later, the children had the best of manners. The king, who was feeling much better, chuckled at their delightful names: Hawk, Sparrow, Robin, Jay, and Dove.

"Our mother and father loved birds," said seven-year-old Jay, who was missing both front teeth.

"It sounds like I would have enjoyed your parents," Prince Eric said gently.

"Rose loves birds, too," said Dove, the littlest, who came over and sat on the prince's lap. He patted her golden hair, which was now washed clean and braided with ribbons.

"So the young woman's name is Rose," the prince said. "Where does she live?"

The children all looked at each other, and then they shrugged their shoulders.

Hawk, the oldest, spoke. "She didn't tell us."

Disappointed but determined, the prince asked another question. "What was she doing at the castle gate?"

Once again, the children thought hard.

"Oh, I remember her saying she needed to go sell her orchids," said thirteen-year-old Sparrow. "She said she had brought them from far away. There was a whole green wagon full of them. Her family counts on the money from the orchids, so she needed to go before the market closed."

Prince Eric leaned forward in his chair, thinking.

"What did she look like?" asked the king.

Sparrow spoke up again. "I remember how she looked. She had long hair just like me. But mine is wavy and brown, and hers was straight and brown. It was tied back with a yellow ribbon. She had a matching yellow-and-white-striped dress. Her eyes were bluish green."

The next morning, Hawk said, "I remember something else about Rose. She wasn't feeling well."

"Hmmm," said Prince Eric. "Let's all take a ride down to the flower market and see what we can find out."

They didn't get much farther than the castle gate when they found a green wagon full of orchids abandoned by the side of the road.

IE

Read to the child: **Let's review. IE can make the long E sound (as in MOVIE). Read the words on the chart. When you get to a word that is a name, point to the animal that you think fits the name best.**

priest	calorie	achieve
brief	relief	shriek
Charlie	diesel	niece

Read to the child: **When the letters I and E together make one sound, like the long E sound, they make a phonogram. However, I and E are not always a phonogram when they are next to each other in a word. Read the following words, in which I makes either the long I sound or the long E sound.**

client	obedient	ingredient
cli ent	o be di ent	in gre di ent
orient	audience	nutrient
or i ent	au di ence	nu tri ent
fortieth	society	twentieth
for ti eth	so ci ety	twen ti eth

Chapter 15: Where Is Rose?

🌿 PARENT/TEACHER

"Oh!" said Dove in her sweet five-year-old voice as her eyes grew misty. "Something must have happened to dear Rose. Why are all of her orchids still here in her wagon?"

A drop of rain hit Prince Eric's nose as he responded. "I don't know, but Rose might need our help. We need to find her."

Prince Eric turned to the carriage driver. "Please take the children back to the castle and ask the king to send some knights into town to ask about Rose. I am going to see if I can find footprints or other clues around the wagon before this rain picks up."

The carriage was soon dashing back to the castle, and another raindrop landed on Prince Eric's head as he searched the wagon. He found a basket with two rolls left in it but nothing else other than the orchids. He looked on the ground for footprints, but the hard, dirt-packed, rocky road didn't hold footprints well. Turning his focus to the roadside by the wagon, he carefully studied the grass and the weeds. Then he spotted it: an area of tall weeds that had been crushed down as though they had been walked on. He followed the half-crushed weeds along until there was an open gate, but there were no more crushed weeds to follow. Up the little path beyond the gate, tucked up in the forest at the end of the path, was a little cottage.

Did she go that way? the prince wondered. *There's only one way to find out.* He sprinted up the path as a misty rain started falling steadily.

The woman who grumpily opened the cottage door after Prince Eric pounded on it was surprised, to say the least, to see the prince standing at her door soaking wet.

She hadn't seen Rose or heard anything about her.

Wondering what to do next, the prince went to the edge of the forest where the cottage was nestled. With his hand held above his eyes as a shield from the rain, he scanned the rolling green hills around him. A tiny flash of yellow among the green caught his eye. Without delay he started running toward that spot. As he got closer, he could tell: Yes! It was a woman in a yellow-and-white dress, propped up against a tree.

"Hello there!" cried Prince Eric when he was close enough for her to hear. Her eyes fluttered open.

"Kind sir! I'm afraid I am very sick and in need of assistance. I saw a cottage. I tried to get there, but I—I was confused and lost my way. I can't walk anymore."

"It's OK," said Eric. "May I carry you?"

Rose nodded.

Prince Eric picked up Rose. "Oh, you're burning up with fever," he said. "I must get you to the castle right away."

"The castle?" Rose mumbled, and then she closed her eyes and fell asleep as Eric started trekking through the misty rain, across the tall, wet grass toward his home.

Prince Eric was seen at a distance by one of the guards on the castle walls, and within minutes, riders on horses came to help. A woman took Rose back to the castle.

"Take her to Mrs. Turner, the castle nurse," Prince Eric said when they got inside the castle. "She needs to get changed into dry clothes. I'll go fetch the doctor myself."

Prince Eric and the king and all five children stayed by Rose's bedside most of the next day. The wound on her leg had quickly been discovered and treated with a powerful healing ointment made from honey and herbs. They kept her fever down by fanning her and applying cold cloths to her head.

They were very quiet so that she could sleep. And she did sleep all day.

"I want her to wake up," whispered Dove as the children left the room for dinner.

"Shhh!!!" said Jay very loudly. "Don't wake her up, Dove!"

Rose's eyes opened. "Dove? Are you here? I remember you. Where am I?"

Dove ran to her side. "You're at the castle. Your leg is infected, so you got a bad fever. Prince Eric found you in the meadow and carried you here."

Rose turned her head ever so slightly to look at Eric, but all her strength was used up. She closed her eyes and fell asleep again.

Around lunchtime the next day, a servant ushered a man into the room. "This man, Michael, claims he is Rose's uncle," the servant explained.

PARENT/TEACHER

"Your Highness," Michael said. "I brought Rose here on my ship and dropped her off to sell her orchids. She was supposed to stay with a family friend for two days until I picked her up. I'm terribly sorry about all of this."

"It's our pleasure to help," said the prince. "We will get a room made up for you. Please stay until she is well."

Mrs. Turner's healing herbs-and-honey blend was successful. Within three days Rose's fever was gone, and her leg was no longer red and swollen.

Early one evening, she was sitting up in bed when Prince Eric and the king were the only ones with her in the room.

STUDENT

"The children have told me all about you," said Prince Eric. "I don't think that there is another young lady as kind as you are in all the kingdom. I'm really glad I met you, and I am so glad you are feeling better."

Rose smiled. "I'm glad I met you, too. And I'm so very grateful for your kindness and your help."

The next morning, the king and Prince Eric found Rose's bed empty, with a note for them lying on the pillow. It read:

> I am so grateful for everything. It's time for me to get home to my parents, who I'm sure have been worried about me. I must apologize to them for causing such worry. ~Forever grateful, Rose

Prince Eric groaned. "Oh, no. We never found out where Rose was from, did we?"

Later that day, the prince rode his horse to the harbor and found out that Michael's ship had left hours ago. There was no sign of it on the horizon.

How will this all end? You'll have to wait to find out. There are yet some mysteries to be discovered and solved. How the Kingdom of Kind got its name and what message the shepherd refused to deliver are still unknown. But for now, let's think about what was started because Rose stopped and helped the children. If she hadn't taken the time to show them kindness, the prince might have never known about her. A magnificent story is now about to unfold. What stories will be started in your own life when you show kindness?

Chapter 16: Practice Page

CH Can Say /sh/

Read to the child: **CH can say /sh/. Read the words.**

chef	machine	Michelle
chaperone	Chicago	Cherilyn

INE Can Say /in/ or /een/

Read to the child: **INE can say /in/. Read the words.**

determine
de term ine

medicine
med i cine

discipline
dis ci pline

Jasmine
Jas mine

Read to the child: **INE can also say /een/. Read each word.**

magazine
mag a zine

sardine
sar dine

chlorine
chlor ine

trampoline
tramp o line

Chapter 16: An Unexpected Surprise

The prince had been researching where all the orchid farms were in the kingdom. It turned out that there was only one, and it was on an island.

It was a bright, beautiful day when Prince Eric, Hawk, Sparrow, Robin, Jay, and Dove boarded a ship to find Rose. The sea sparkled as if it were covered in tiny diamonds. Bright-white gulls soared against the deep-blue sky as they circled around the departing ship.

Can you guess how things turned out when Prince Eric and the children arrived on the island? Well, things didn't go as Prince Eric had hoped. Remember Rose's mother, Tibby, who used to be the baker at the castle? She shrieked in terror when she saw the prince walking up the pathway to her farm. She slammed her cottage door and refused to allow Prince Eric inside.

"No tyrant who was that selfish and conceited could ever change!" Tibby declared. "He thinks only of himself. Surely he is deceiving everyone. Surely he is up to some kind of mischief."

🌱 **PARENT/TEACHER**

Tibby and her husband refused to leave the cottage until the prince left. The prince was considerate and asked if he could stay and help on the island if he slept on the ship, and Tibby's husband agreed to this arrangement.

So for many days, the prince slept on his ship at night and worked long, laborious hours on the orchid farm during the day, whistling and singing. He watered the orchids. He diligently weeded the vegetable and herb gardens. He milked the cows and left fresh milk in a pail on the cottage doorstep. He patched the stable ceiling. He meticulously trimmed trees and bushes. He even built a fence to keep wild goats away from the orchid fields. On the steep, grassy hillside, he collected wildflowers and left them on the doorstep along with notes of apology to Tibby.

Rose and the children helped Eric each day. In the evenings, they sang songs and hymns outside Tibby's cottage. Each day Rose would ask her parents to give the prince a chance, but they refused to leave the cottage.

Tibby watched out the window every day. She was shocked! She could not conceive any reason why the prince was doing these kind things. Finally one day, she opened the window as the prince was passing by.

"Why are you here? What are you doing all of this for? Why won't you leave?" she called.

The prince smiled and replied, "I have searched the kingdom high and low for you. I wanted to apologize for being so conceited and cruel, and I especially wanted to apologize for never thanking you for your service."

Tibby finally realized that the prince was honest and sincere, so she invited him to the cottage for dinner.

For the next few weeks, Eric and Rose spent most of their time together, going for long walks in the fields, playing with the children, and even doing their chores together. Prince Eric knew he was falling in love with Rose and that she was the one with the beautiful character he was searching for in a wife.

Six months later, Eric and Rose were married. The next day, they adopted the five orphaned children. Two weeks after that, Eric's father died contentedly with the knowledge that Eric had learned the keys to happiness and that these keys of gratitude, service, and work had brought so much joy to their lives and glory to God. Eric then began to reign as the king.

One winter evening, a few weeks after King Eric began his reign, Rose and Eric sat drinking peppermint tea and reading in the vast castle library by the glow of a bright candle. Outside, the snow made a picturesque scene as it blanketed the world in white.

Eric was still determined to find some information about the mysterious two kings who first ruled the Kingdom of Kind. With any leisure time they had, the determined couple scoured the books in the library. But they could not find a single word written about the two kings.

Suddenly, Rose jumped. "What is that?" she shrieked as she pointed out the window. "Do you see that moving silhouette?"

"It looks like a man in a long, dark cloak sneaking around at the edge of the garden," replied King Eric as he stood up abruptly. "Guards! There is a mysterious man in the garden. He may be a thief. Please capture him and bring him to me immediately."

Within five minutes the guards had brought the mysterious man to the king. The man looked fatigued and wore a tattered, unique-looking cloak.

"Who are you?" inquired the king gently, but firmly.

The man gestured toward the guards. "I will tell you as soon as you excuse your guards," said the man. "You will not want them to hear what I have to say."

"Very well," replied Eric. "You are tied up and can do no harm."

Eric excused the guards and then turned toward the man. With his roped hands, the stranger pushed off his hood, revealing his face. King Eric stood abruptly and gasped. He had met this man before. It was the shepherd who had shared the cave with him and Milo.

Chapter 17: Practice Page

🔊 **PHONICS**

Decoding

Read to the child: **Say the sound of each phonogram in the green boxes.** Hints are below each box if needed.

ph	qu	wh	wr	ir	dge
phone	quit	white	wrap	bird	fudge

INE Can Say /in/ or /een/

Read to the child: **INE can say /een/. Read each word.**

magazine	gasoline

chlorine	marine
CH can say /k/	A can say /uh/

Read to the child: **INE can also say /in/. Read each word in the boxes.**

determine	intestine
Jasmine	medicine
examine	discipline

🔤 **VOCABULARY**

Read the following information to the child:

Aghast means greatly shocked.

I was aghast when I saw a tornado in the distance.

Chapter 17: The Shepherd's Message

"It's you!" cried King Eric to the shepherd. "I can't believe it! Let me take those ropes off your hands."

The shepherd looked at King Eric with just as much surprise. "You are the king? You were the young man in the cave, weren't you?"

Eric untied the man as he spoke. "Yes, I'm the king now. I was the prince when I met you, but I didn't feel it was right to reveal my identity at that time. I hope you understand."

With the ropes now untied, King Eric gestured kindly toward a chair.

"Please sit down. You must be exhausted from your long journey. You told me in the cave that you live in a faraway land?"

Gratefully, the man sank into a chair by the fireplace. "Yes, I'm from Rayliftn, a few weeks' journey from here."

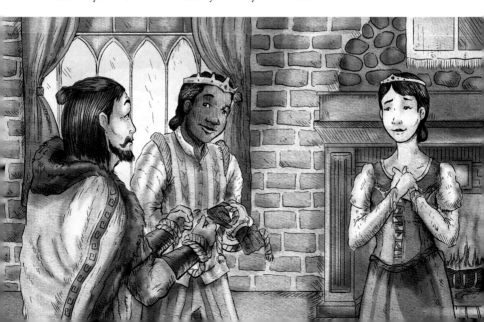

"What is your name, kind sir?" Rose asked.

"Oh, I apologize. I forgot to introduce you to my wife, Rose," King Eric said.

The shepherd stood and bowed slightly to Rose. "It's a pleasure to meet you, Your Majesty. My name is Gerold."

"You must be hungry," Rose said. "We, of course, are curious to hear why you are here, but why don't we have some food brought to you first?"

"Thank you," said Gerold. "That is very generous of you."

Rose had warm brown bread, slices of pale yellow cheese, a bowl of spicy stew, and a steaming cup of hot cinnamon tea brought to Gerold in the library.

"Before I give you my message, could I hear your story, King Eric?" requested the shepherd. "News of your change of heart finally reached my kingdom, and that is why I am here, but I would love to know how it all happened."

"Of course!" said King Eric.

Just then Hawk, Sparrow, Robin, Jay, and Dove entered the room. They had just taken baths and were in their nightclothes.

The children were given permission to stay and listen as King Eric and Queen Rose told their story. The flames in the fireplace danced and crackled merrily. Outside, the snow fell quietly, with big feathery flakes swirling in the sighing breeze. Dove snuggled up on King Eric's lap, and Jay and Robin sat in front of Rose's chair on the big rug, laying their heads against her legs.

When Rose started telling the part of the story where she met the children, they all piped up and wanted to tell what they remembered. Patiently, Rose gave each child a turn to tell part of the story.

"And that is how it all happened," said King Eric as he finished the story.

"And you have never found the peasant whose cart you set on fire?" asked the shepherd. "I remember you telling me about that in the cave and how you wished you could find the man."

King Eric shook his head. "No, I never found him. I still remember what he looks like, though, and I hope one day we will cross paths."

It had taken so long to tell the story that Dove had fallen asleep in King Eric's lap. The snow had stopped, and the sky had cleared. Bright stars twinkled in a sea of black outside the large library window.

"Please excuse us as we put the children to bed," Rose said. "Then we would love to hear your message."

"Can't I stay up and listen?" asked Hawk.

Before Rose could answer, Gerold spoke. "This message is of supreme importance, and it will be quite shocking, I fear. I think it's advisable for only the king and queen to hear my message, and then they can decide what to do with the information that I share."

After the queen and king put their children to bed, they found the shepherd pacing the library, holding a scroll in his hand.

"I must give you my message now," Gerold said.

"And then won't you stay in a guest room tonight?" inquired Rose.

With a shake of his head, Gerold declined the offer. "I have a room at an inn, and I will leave for my journey home right at sunrise. Please sit down. I will begin."

With a pounding heart, King Eric sat down. *What could this message be?* he wondered.

Gerold held up the scroll. "I have a message for you from the second king of Kind."

Eric drew in his breath with astonishment. He was aghast. "But the second king of this kingdom died long, long before I was born."

"Yes, but he wrote a message for you before he died."

"That is utterly impossible," cried Eric. "How could he have even known who I am if I wasn't yet born?"

"I suppose I should start from the beginning," replied Gerold.

"Please do," said Eric, moving to the edge of his chair.

Gerold took in a deep breath and began his story. "I come from a long line of shepherds from the Kingdom of Rayliftn. My fifth great-grandfather, Gabriel, was tending his flocks one day when the second king of the Kingdom of Kind, King Viridian, came to him. Evidently, the king had been watching Gabriel for several days before he approached him. The king had come to find a stranger in a far-off land whom he could trust. Apparently, the king knew something was about to happen to him."

"Wait," said Rose. "I want to make sure I'm following what you are saying. The second king of the Kingdom of Kind, King Viridian, traveled all the way to your kingdom because he knew something was going to happen to him, and he came to your ancestor, Gabriel, a shepherd?"

"That's right," said Gerold. "King Viridian didn't know my fifth great-grandfather. He just wanted to find someone far from his kingdom who was humble and trustworthy. King Viridian gave my ancestor a scroll, and he told him to hand the scroll down from generation to generation until the Kingdom of Kind had a ruler who was humble and caring."

The shepherd fingered the old, worn scroll in his hands as he continued. "This scroll has been handed down from parent to child in my family line. We have each been entrusted to keep the scroll until a king from your kingdom was kind and caring. None of the kings since King Viridian have been humble and caring . . . until you. When we first met, I had come to check if the king was kind, but found that he was not. I didn't receive the news that he had changed until after he died. So now, it is my duty to give this scroll to you."

The shepherd then took a big breath, held out the scroll, and said, "I must prepare you for one thing." Gerold bowed his head and whispered quietly, "You are not actually the rightful king of this kingdom."

 **PHONICS**

Decoding

Read to the child: **Read the words with sounds of EA.**

ea	deal, realization, appearance, disease
	thread, measurement, pleasure, dread
	steak, groundbreaking, yea, greatly

Say the sound of each phonogram in the green boxes. Hints are below each box if needed.

oy	igh	wh	ir	ph	ur
b<u>oy</u>	h<u>igh</u>	<u>wh</u>ite	b<u>ir</u>d	<u>ph</u>one	t<u>ur</u>n

CH Can Say /k/ or /sh/

Read to the child: **CH can say /k/ or /sh/. Read each word. For words with a phonogram circled, say the sound of the phonogram, and then read the whole word.**

brochure

mechanic

technical

echoed

chaperone

Charlene

 **VOCABULARY**

Read the following information to the child:

A **chasm** is a deep hole or opening in the ground, ice, or rock.
   A bridge was built over the chasm.

Chapter 18: The Scroll

After handing the scroll to King Eric, Gerold the shepherd put his hand on King Eric's shoulder and looked into the king's face intently. "May you be blessed," he said before slipping out into the cold night, leaving the king and queen alone in the library.

For a while the couple sat in shocked silence, amazement filling their minds. The winter wind whistled softly outside the window, and the soft crackling and popping of the fire in the fireplace echoed across the stone walls of the library as if it were a vast, lonely canyon.

Eric's thoughts spun and circled like the snowflakes that had started falling again outside. He held the ancient scroll in his hand, but he did not dare open it.

"I feel that everything may change when I read this," he whispered. "I feel as if I were standing at one end of a bridge spanning a mighty chasm, and when I walk across this bridge, I will never be able to return to the other side."

Rose put her warm, comforting arms around her husband as she whispered, "For so long you have wished to know about the first two kings who ruled this kingdom, and now you are holding the words of one of them—King Viridian. He wrote these words for you. Don't fear walking across this bridge, for I shall walk with you, and I will stay right by your side, no matter where the bridge leads. Yes, we are commencing on a new journey— an unknown journey—but it cannot be helped. We must have courage."

Eric hugged his wife and nodded his agreement. Taking in a deep breath, he opened the scroll and began to read:

My name is King Viridian, and I am the son of King Kind, the first king of the kingdom. If you are reading this scroll, you probably have not heard of me. To explain, I must start from the beginning of the story.

My father founded this kingdom. He helped hundreds of people escape from a far-off land ruled by a tyrant. He led the group for two months through the forest and mountains until they arrived in this beautiful land. The people asked my father to be the first king.

Because he was so good and gentle and generous, the people named him King Kind, and the kingdom was named the Kingdom of Kind.

My father and mother wanted a large family, but they were blessed with only one child—me. My father named me Viridian because it is the name of his favorite color—a shade of green that reminded him of the mighty, ancient trees in our forest. When I was a boy, he always told me, "Son, you were designed to be like these trees, having strong roots and growing noble and straight, reaching up to our Creator in the heavens."

When my father died, I tried to follow his example in all I did. Our kingdom thrived, and our people gained a reputation all over the world for being kind and generous. I loved to write, and I encouraged the writing of good and beautiful poetry, stories, and books. Our kingdom had more books than any kingdom in history.

Unfortunately, darkness was growing in the heart of a cruel man: Tiff, the head of my army.

He was once a good man, but he became jealous of me, and, as jealousy can do if left unchecked, it changed him into a bitter man without any honor or civility left inside him.

He stopped listening to his conscience, and his heart became hard and cold.

But our kingdom was peaceful. We had no reason to use the army, so I hardly had occasion to work with Tiff.

Finally, it came to my attention that Tiff had been poisoning the minds of the soldiers with deceitful lies for years. They had a scheme to make Tiff the king. I investigated and found that I didn't have one loyal soldier in my army—they all supported Tiff.

I immediately released Tiff from his duties with the army. He laughed and said that I did not have the authority to release him from that position. Rather, he would soon be releasing me from my position. I was stunned.

Secretly, I followed him when he left, and I overheard a discussion he was having with three men. These men had come from the land named Gorg, from which my father had escaped before he founded this kingdom. They were discussing their final plot for Tiff to become king.

You see, I had not yet had any children to inherit the throne.

Tiff and his men planned to capture my wife and me that very day, take us as prisoners to the land of Gorg, tell the people of our kingdom that my wife and I had been drowned at sea, and present them with a forged document naming Tiff as the king should anything happen to me.

Once Tiff became king, he planned to destroy all records of the history of our kingdom so generations to come would not remember my father or me.

As quickly as possible, I returned to the castle, threw money and jewels into a knapsack, and slipped secretly out of the kingdom with my wife.

We have traveled far, and I have decided to give this scroll to a trustworthy shepherd.

I do not yet know how to save my kingdom, but my heart tells me that Tiff and his men may succeed in their plot. And if they do, Tiff will wipe out all knowledge of me, so eventually, I will not even be remembered.

But he will not know about this secret scroll. I will ask the shepherd to have the scroll handed down from generation to generation until a king with a good heart reigns in the Kingdom of Kind. Only then will things be set right.

What Tiff doesn't know is that my wife is expecting a baby in five months. We have not told anyone. If we are not able to take the kingdom back, Tiff and his men will hunt my wife and me the whole world over with relentless vigor until we are found and captured. Our baby will never be safe.

We don't know what will happen, but if we can stay hidden until the baby is born, we have a plan. To protect the baby from being captured, we will leave him or her on the doorstep of a humble but noble young couple I know who lives on a remote island in our kingdom.

For their safety and the baby's, we cannot let the couple know who the baby is or who left the baby there. But if it is a boy, I will carve a small wooden tree to leave in the basket with the baby. If it is a girl, I will leave a carved flower. The carving will say "Always be kind" on it. I will leave a note explaining that the tree or the flower is from the child's birth parents and should be kept safe and handed down through the generations.

In order for you to find the true heir to the kingdom, simply send a proclamation throughout the kingdom asking if anyone has a carved tree or carved flower that has been handed down from generation to generation. Then check the carving for the words "Always be kind."

I desire that my posterity will be able to rule this kingdom again. I know that a good ruler would never accept the crown if he or she weren't really the rightful heir, so I trust you will do the morally correct thing and find the true king or queen. Thank you for your help.

King Viridian

Decoding

Read to the child: **Point to each box and say the sound of the phonogram.**

ir	oa	ai	au	ay	wr
b<u>ir</u>d	<u>oa</u>t	p<u>ai</u>d	p<u>au</u>se	d<u>ay</u>	<u>wr</u>ite

Read the words with different sounds of OU.

ou	surround, counsel, pronounce, foundation
	wound, coupon, crouton, routine
	couple, southern, touchdown, encourage
our	our can say /or/: pour, court, mourn

TU and TURE

Read to the child: **TU can say /ch/. Read the words with TURE, which says /chur/.**

frac**ture**	cap**ture**	struc**ture**
mois**ture**	pic**ture**	lec**ture**
fea**ture**	mix**ture**	pas**ture**

Chapter 19: Meeting in the Forest

PARENT/TEACHER

When Eric finished reading the scroll aloud, he and Rose were dumbfounded.

"Unbelievable!" Eric exclaimed quietly. "I—I am not the rightful king. I truly am not. I am not a king at all. This castle does not belong to me. My sixth great-grandfather was Tiff—a deceitful traitor. I'm not sure I know who I am anymore."

Rose stood abruptly. "You know exactly who you are, Eric: a kind, compassionate, hardworking, thoughtful man. This does not at all change who you are. No, you are not the rightful king, but you did not know that until now. And you are not at all like Tiff."

Late into the night, Eric wrestled with his feelings. They felt as gnarled as the trunk of the big oak tree behind the castle. Although he lay nestled between the smooth silk sheets in his broad, ornately carved bed, he felt as if he were sleeping in a bed of thistles. He realized that he had indeed crossed a bridge and could never go back. Tossing and turning, his mind whirled until he was finally so exhausted that he fell into a much-needed sleep.

The gentle morning sunlight wrapped him in a warm golden glow and slowly woke him up. Eric sat up as he recalled the events of the previous evening. The new day felt hopeful, like a breath of fresh air. A smile slowly spread across Eric's face.

Eric turned to Rose, who had just woken up.

"I don't need to be the king," Eric stated excitedly. "I have more important titles that can never be taken from me: husband, father, friend, and child of God. I don't need to be a king to be happy. After all, the three keys to happiness that I found while staying with Peter and his family have nothing to do with being king. Anyone can use those keys in any situation, and that is exactly what I am going to do. I cannot wait to venture into this new period of my life. We must tell the children."

Before their normal morning routine, Rose and Eric took their children out to the castle's southern pasture where they couldn't be overheard. As they sat on some tree stumps in the pasture, which was blanketed with snow, the children learned that they were no longer going to be princes and princesses.

Just as Rose and Eric thought, the children responded well to the news.

"We are a family," said ten-year-old Robin, who always wore her hair in a braided crown. "Royal or not, we will always have each other."

"Well, I still *feel* like a princess," said little Dove.

Eric ruffled Dove's hair. "I hope you will always feel like a princess, Dove. You are so special because of who you are inside, not because of a title."

"Where will we live?" asked Jay, his seven-year-old mind trying to imagine how their lives might change. "Can we go live with Milo and Dune? We should write them a letter today and see if we can go there." They had loved hearing stories of Milo so much that they felt like they knew him.

Rose laughed. "That would be fun, Jay! But we can't just stop being the king and queen right now. The kingdom would turn into chaos."

"But what if the heir cannot be found?" asked Sparrow, twisting her long hair.

Eric had not considered that possibility. Could he really go on being the king, knowing he was not the rightful ruler? That seemed just as hard as having to leave the castle.

"And what will we do if the rightful heir is a horrid person or is very lazy?" asked Dove with big eyes.

Eric had not considered that possibility either.

"We will take everything one day at a time, children," he said. "Right now, let's go have breakfast."

Over a meal of gourmet cocoa, warm vanilla scones, and golden croissants, Eric looked out on the acres of beautiful gardens that surrounded the castle. He ached inside, knowing that he would need to leave his beloved castle, its library, and its orchards when the true ruler was found, but he did not dwell on his sorrow.

After Eric consulted more with Rose and the children, they all decided it was best to tell no one that Eric was not the true king until the rightful heir was found. But they would waste no time in trying to find that heir.

That evening, Eric wrote an epistle. Rose and the children made copies of it, and then Eric's knights posted the epistle in the town square of every village in the kingdom.

> By order of King Eric, anyone in possession of a carved wooden tree or flower handed down from his or her ancestors is to bring it to the castle. If it is the one we seek, an invaluable treasure will be yours.

Chapter 20: Practice Page

GUE Can Say /g/

Read to the child: **GUE can say /g/.** In the words with a red letter I, the I says the long E sound. Read the words.

intrigue	fatigue	dialogue
league	plague	tongue

INE Can Say /in/ or /een/

Read to the child: **INE can say /in/.** Read the words.

determine	feminine
doctrine	margarine

Read to the child: **INE can also say /een/.** Read each word.

trampoline	Josephine
glycine Y says the long I sound	routine OU can say /ew/

Read the following information to the child:

Loathsome means disgusting and unpleasant.

We plugged our noses as a loathsome smell filled the air.

Chapter 20: Is the Heir Found?

PARENT/TEACHER

Eric's heart was pounding like someone banging steadily on a door. His epistle had been delivered to the people of his kingdom the evening before, just as the sun was setting. Now the morning sun had barely emerged from behind the low hills, and a servant had just informed Eric that a man was waiting in the main entryway—a man with a carved flower.

"I'm about to meet the rightful king!" Eric exclaimed to Rose as he hurriedly put on his vest and jacket. "Although I was hoping we would find the king, I am astounded that he came so quickly. Actually, I wondered if he would come at all."

"I have been wondering the same thing," said Rose. "There would be no carved flower or carved tree that said 'Always be kind' on it if King Viridian was unsuccessful in leaving his baby on someone's doorstep. And what if the flower or tree was not handed down or was lost? It has been a very long time since Tiff took over the kingdom. But now, if this man really has this carved flower or tree, it appears that King Viridian did leave his baby on some humble peasant's doorstep in our kingdom and that the carving was handed down through his family."

"I know!" exclaimed King Eric. "I'm so anxious that I can hardly bring myself to open these doors and meet this man, but I'm determined to move forward."

Rose smiled and gave Eric a gentle nudge. "Our curiosity is about to turn into knowledge. Let's go!"

Eric pushed open the ornately carved wooden door, and the couple entered the spacious entryway.

A man with long, greasy black hair; a sharp nose; beady black eyes; and a crooked smile bowed deeply.

"Your Majesty," he began in a coarse, unpleasant voice, "it seems I have something of interest to you." The man's shrewd eyes narrowed. "But I am intrigued. Why would the king want my family heirloom—an antique of immeasurable worth to my beloved family? And what makes you think that I am just going to hand over something so precious? I demand to know the reward before I show the item to you. Perhaps I may need to request more than what you are offering in exchange for my carving."

Eric was aghast and dismayed. His thoughts were swimming, and he felt an agonizing pit in his stomach. How could he let this loathsome man rule the kingdom? He turned to Rose, whose jaw had dropped. Neither of them could utter a word.

Eric's mind raced. *What should I do?* he thought. *I only want to do the right thing, but I am not sure what the right thing is in this situation.*

The man reached into his pocket and pulled out a leather pouch. "It's in here," he said. "Tell me the treasure you are offering in exchange for my item."

Eric uttered a silent prayer and felt a gentle peace come over him. He took a deep breath, collected his thoughts, and said calmly, "Sir, we are not going to take the item from you. If it is the item we are looking for, you will be able to keep it and receive the treasure. Has this item been handed down by your ancestors?"

"Of course," replied the man with a sneer as he handed the pouch to Eric.

STUDENT

Eric pulled a dirty miniature wooden carving out of the pouch and examined it. It was roughly cut, but it did resemble a flower.

"Is it authentic?" whispered Rose so quietly that Eric could scarcely hear her.

Eric turned the carving over and over in his hands, searching for the words "Always be kind." There were no words carved anywhere.

"I'm afraid," said Eric in utter relief, "that this is not the authentic carving for which we are searching."

A few hours later, an astoundingly long line of people stretched like a long snake from the castle gates to the village center.

Each person clutched a carving of a flower or tree, and each person claimed that the carving had been handed down by his or her ancestors.

"Are they all dishonest, scheming scoundrels?" Rose asked sadly as she watched the people arguing and jostling each other roughly as they tried to cut in line. "I'm sure all those flowers and trees were carved this morning."

Eric sighed. "Yes, but perhaps one person in the line is the rightful ruler. We must check each carving."

And so they did. One by one, the carvings proved inauthentic—there were no words carved into any of them.

The last person in line was an old woman with greedy eyes. "This is what you are looking for!" she cried as she thrust a poorly carved wooden flower into Eric's hands.

"No," said Eric with a sigh after examining the flower and finding no words on it. "It is not."

The old woman hobbled away angrily. Eric and Rose were left with only the sound of a sharp winter wind banging on the castle windows as if demanding to be let in.

The family felt quite fatigued as they ate a late dinner at the long banquet table that night. Just as they started eating dessert crepes, a servant entered the room.

"There is a young man here to see you, King Eric," the man said with a bow. "He says he has traveled from afar."

Eric sighed. "I suppose I shall go see him. It's probably someone else who is trying to deceive me."

But it wasn't someone trying to deceive the king. It was Milo and his dog, Dune!

"I haven't visited you since you became the king!" Milo declared. "I'm fifteen now, and Aunt Cassandra said I was old enough to journey on my own to see you."

"I'm not really the king, Milo," King Eric said before he realized that he had given away his secret.

Chapter 21: Practice Page

Decoding

Read to the child: **Read the words with sounds of EA.**

ea	measles, fearsome, seamstress, seasonal
	threaten, deaf, readily, farmstead, jealous
	steak, groundbreaking, greatly

Read to the child: **EAR can say /air/ and /er/. Read the words.**

ear	pear, swear, tear, bearable, wearable
	earthquake, research, rehearse, yearn

Say the sound of each phonogram in the green boxes. Hints are below each box if needed.

wr	igh	wh	oa	ph	oi
write	high	white	boat	phone	boil

☀ Challenging Words ☀

Read the words repeatedly until you can read them all without help.

omelet

croissant

theory

silhouette

crepes

dungeon

conquer

pistachio

Chapter 21: Journey to See Cassandra

"You're not really the king?" Milo asked in surprise.

Eric looked around and then sighed in relief. No servants seemed to be within earshot.

"Come," said Eric, taking Milo gently by the arm. "Let's go on a walk while I tell you a story, but you must not tell others. The safety and peace of the kingdom depend upon it."

As the sun slid behind the mountains, turning the sky yellow with a bit of pink blush, Eric told Milo the whole story, emphasizing again how important it was not to share the information.

They had just turned around on the forest trail to head back to the castle. Milo gasped. "Wait! Cassandra has a little carved tree in her home. It's the size of my hand, and it's on her dresser. She even has it on a little stand. It looks really nice and newly painted, but it could still be old underneath the new paint. Oh, do you think that maybe Cassandra is the heir?"

"Milo, that would be amazing if she were. I have longed for the heir to be someone good and kind, and there are so few good and kind people in this kingdom."

"Maybe we should write her a letter and ask her about it?" Milo suggested.

Eric thought for a moment. "No, we can get there as fast as a letter, and then we don't have to wait for a letter to be returned."

"Wahoo! Wahoo! Wahoo!" cried Dove as she danced around the room like a little bird after Eric announced that the whole family was going back with Milo to visit his home.

"While we are there, can we see the cave where you met the shepherd?" asked Hawk.

"I think so!" replied Eric. "But first, we will go to Cassandra's home. I can hardly wait to see if her tree has the words 'Always be kind' carved on it."

Sparrow, always the one to think logically and maturely, asked many questions. "Would Cassandra even want to be the queen? Would she be a good ruler? How would the people feel about a woman from a remote island that raises llamas suddenly ruling the kingdom?"

"All good questions, Sparrow!" exclaimed Eric. "I guess we'll find out!"

"Oh!" cried Robin. "I just thought of something. If Cassandra moves here into the castle to rule the kingdom, her house will be empty. We could live there and make llama-wool ropes!"

King Eric raised his eyebrows. "Umm, maybe."

The beginning of the journey on the ship was exciting and pleasant. They experienced good weather, made friends with the crew, and had endless fun playing with Dune. However, on the last day, a stowaway was discovered—a man in a black cloak hiding behind some barrels. The crew brought him out to the deck, and Eric instantly recognized the long, greasy hair; the sharp nose; and the beady black eyes.

"Your Majesty," the man said when he looked over at Eric and made a rather mocking bow.

Eric also recognized the man's coarse, unpleasant voice.

The man sneered. "Actually, should I call you King Eric or . . . just plain Eric?"

"What?" exclaimed Rose, who was standing next to Eric.

"Oh," said the man. "It's just that I heard something on the trail by the castle. I was just enjoying a little stroll in the forest. I heard the whole story—the shepherd, the scroll."

"What is he talking about?" asked the ship's captain.

"I'm talking about him not being the real king!" cried the man. He pulled something from his cloak and held it up. "And I have this to prove it!"

Eric gasped again. It was the scroll. He had left it locked in his desk drawer. Somehow, this man had stolen it. Before Eric could say anything, the king's soldiers charged toward the man, knocking him down and sending the scroll flying into the air and over the railing.

Everyone ran to the railing and saw the scroll sinking below the surface of the sea.

The man in the black cloak looked around. A populated island was not too far off, maybe a ten-minute swim. They had been traveling around the island's large coast. Without another thought, the man jumped over the railing and plunged into the ocean.

Eric hardly breathed as he watched the scroll sink down into the water well before the man could get to it.

The man splashed the water. "No!"

"Give him a lifeboat," cried Eric. "It may be farther to land than he can swim with all his clothes on."

The crew was reluctant, as they didn't want to help the man, but they also didn't dare disobey the king's orders. They lowered a lifeboat and let it splash into the water.

The white sails of the ship billowed wide with air as a sudden wind arose. The wind pushed the ship quickly across the water, away from the man. King Eric watched as the man climbed into the lifeboat and soon became just a speck in the distance.

"Oh!" cried Dove, climbing into Eric's arms. "That was not a nice man."

"Do you think he is still going to try to prove that you are not the rightful king?" Robin asked.

Eric smiled cheerfully. "He might, but don't worry, Robin. Without the scroll, no one will believe him. Besides, if we find the rightful heir soon, then it really won't matter."

Rose then hugged Eric. "I'm glad all is well now."

The island on which Cassandra lived was just as Eric remembered. The high mountains shot into the air and covered most of the island. However, this time, Eric was more prepared. Most notably, he had shoes that were not made of ferns. Also, he had brought two donkeys on the ship, and now they loaded them with saddlebags containing supplies.

Accompanied by four soldiers, the happy group made its way up through the mountains. Dove and Jay rode the donkeys most of the time, but they also gave Robin and Sparrow turns riding.

The first night, they all camped beneath the stars next to a large campfire, the soldiers taking turns keeping watch. Other than wolves howling in the distance, it was a peaceful night.

After traveling most of the next day, the group arrived in Cassandra's valley and soon ended its journey at her home. A surprised but happy Cassandra welcomed them heartily. King Eric allowed the soldiers to go nap in the barn. Rose asked if Cassandra's twins and Milo could take Hawk, Sparrow, Robin, Jay, and Dove up to the llama pens while the adults spoke. Finally, Eric and Rose were alone with Cassandra, and Eric could not contain his curiosity anymore.

"Cassandra, you probably haven't seen the epistle that I sent out to my kingdom. We are looking for a small carved tree or flower that has been handed down from an ancestor. Do you have such an item?"

"Why, yes, I do," said Cassandra. "I have a carved tree."

"Where did you get it?" asked Eric excitedly.

"My father gave it to me before my husband died. I'll go get it."

Chapter 22: Practice Page

Y in the Middle of a Word

Read to the child: **Y can make the short I sound (as in SIT) in the middle of a word. Read the words on the chart. In each row of words, clap after you read a word that has to do with music.**

pyramid	myth	hymn
mystery	lyric	oxygen
rhythm	symbolic	symptom
symphony	system	crystal

Read to the child: **Y can make the long I sound (as in LINE) in the middle of a word. Read the words on the chart.**

rhyme	python	cycle
hydrate	style	recycle

IE

Read to the child: **IE can make the long E sound (as in MOVIE). Read the words on the chart.**

chief	grieve	grief
niece	series	brownie

Chapter 22: A Surprise

Cassandra slipped into her bedroom and came out holding a beautiful but small carved wooden tree with a thick trunk and broad branches.

"The paint on the front was worn and chipped," explained Cassandra, "so I repainted it last year." She handed the item to Eric and continued speaking. "My grandfather was a gifted wood carver, and he made this for my father. My father gave it to me years ago."

"Oh," said Eric, trying not to sound disappointed as he learned that the tree had not been handed down for many generations. He also saw that there was no writing carved into the tree. "It's really beautiful," he said as he handed it back to Cassandra. "But unfortunately, it's not the item we are looking for."

The family enjoyed a few days of peace and friendship with Cassandra and her family as they helped around the farm, told stories around the fireplace, and learned how to make llama-wool ropes. Then Eric and Rose felt anxious to return home.

Normally so cheerful, Eric felt a bit downtrodden after returning home from Cassandra's island. It was hard to perform the duties of being a king now that he knew he was not the rightful heir. He felt like an imposter. Yet he couldn't just stop ruling.

Two weeks after his return, Eric sat at a desk in his office next to a big window, writing slowly on smooth paper with his quill pen. Ever since Peter and his son, Nathan, had taught Eric how to recognize and appreciate beauty, Eric had started writing down his observations and feelings in the form of poetry and stories that he delighted his children with at bedtime.

STUDENT

His pen scratched in the quiet room as he wrote these words:

Who I Am

I wear a crown, a symbol of high authority.
And yet I am not the king; it's such a mystery.
I sit here, and I analyze what I ought to do,
But after all my analysis, I still don't have a clue.
I'm happy to be any note in God's symphony
If I could only know what note that ought to be.

Suddenly, a voice interrupted Eric's writing. "May I see what you are writing?"

Eric whirled around and couldn't believe his eyes.

There stood Peter in his thick winter traveling cloak, a bright smile spread across his kind face. Eric couldn't have been more grateful to see anyone. Ever since Eric had been shipwrecked and taken in by Peter and his family, Peter had been like a father to Eric.

That evening the servants prepared a wonderful dinner in celebration of Peter's visit. Eric, Rose, their children, and Peter entered the dining hall. Happy laughter and voices were dancing and echoing off the stone walls.

The group observed and discussed the paintings hanging in the room while they waited for the dinner to be served. Eric was reminded of how much he loved Peter's deep laugh and his twinkling, merry eyes.

"How is your family?" Eric asked.

"Oh," replied Peter, "we've had hard times. A violent storm hit our island last month. It sounded like a group of rhinoceroses stampeding our home. Unfortunately, the storm damaged our home quite extensively."

Eric put his hand on Peter's shoulder. "I'm so sorry to hear that news. Yet you look so merry and happy."

"Well, it's just wood and glass windows—just things. It's been a lot of hard, physical work to do the repairs, but we are very well and happy."

The food was ready, so the group found their way to the long table.

As Eric pulled out his chair to sit down, he noticed a beautifully made but worn carving of a tree in the middle of his dinner plate. He picked it up, turned it over, and read the carved words "Always be kind." Eric let out a cry so loud that instantly a hush fell over the room.

Rose ran over to Eric, and he gently placed the authentic carving into her hand, and she, too, let out a cry after seeing the carved words.

"Who . . . where . . . how?" Eric was so astounded that he couldn't utter a complete sentence.

ON, ION, and EON

Read to the child: **Read the words on the chart in which ON, ION, or EON says /en/, /un/, or /yen/. Note that SS can say /sh/.**

skeleton	fashion	on**ion**
cushion	mission	cotton
passion	un**ion**	possession
session	expression	rebell**ion**

CH can say /sh/

Read to the child: **Read the words in which CH says /sh/:** Chicago, pistachio, chute, chevron.

✦ Challenging Words ✦

Read the words repeatedly until you can read them all without help.

coupon

meringue

machine

spaghetti

suite

rhinoceros

Chapter 23: The True Heir Reigns

Eric again looked down at the carved tree in his hand. "Whose tree is this?" he cried.

"It is mine," said Peter softly.

"Peter! It's yours?"

"Yes, I saw the epistle posted at our town square. I'm sorry I could not come and bring it until now. I couldn't travel because of the storms we have had."

"Please, tell me how you got this tree," Eric asked.

"Well," started Peter, "this tree was given to me by my father. It was given to my father by his father, and so on. My father told me that the tree was placed in a basket with my fifth great-grandfather when he was left on a doorstep. It was accompanied by a note asking that the tree be handed down from father to his firstborn child. The tree has obviously been a mystery to our family, but it has also been a very precious item to us. The words on the tree, 'Always be kind,' have inspired me and pushed me to follow that counsel. I cannot conceive of any reason you would want the tree, but I know it must be important. However, if it is possible, I would like to keep the carving so I can pass it down to my son. I don't need any treasure. The life I have is wonderful, and I'm contented. My wife and family are all the treasure I need."

Silence reigned in the dining hall. Finally, Eric stood up. He could not contain the huge smile spreading across his face.

"This is truly unbelievable!" exclaimed Eric. "It's perfect! It couldn't be better!"

Ten minutes later, Eric finished telling Peter about King Viridian and the scroll.

Tears were streaming down Peter's face. Then he bowed his head. "I—I cannot be the king. I'm just an ordinary man. I don't even want to be the king."

"You are not an ordinary man," Eric asserted. "No one is ordinary unless he chooses to be. As a humble farmer, you did much good for those around you. As the king, you could do much good for many more people. You cannot evade this responsibility; you *are* the rightful heir to the throne."

Seven days later, an epistle was posted in every village explaining that Peter was the rightful king. Eric passed the crown to King Peter in a public ceremony and celebration, and Peter began ruling.

Eric, Rose, and their children moved to the beautiful island where Rose's parents lived. A mile from Rose's parents' home, Eric built a charming cottage on a grassy knoll overlooking the vast blue ocean. Rose's father was too old and sick to work, so Eric happily ran the orchid farm.

Milo came to visit them in their new home.

"How does it feel to no longer be a king?" Milo asked him as they worked together to water rows of orchids.

"I'm very contented, Milo," Eric responded. "I get to work with the fragrant flowers and the rich soil; I love having time to teach, play with, and tell stories to my sweet children; and I love visiting my mother-in-law, Tibby, who has become my great friend. As I've told you before, she bakes amazing rolls, and I get to have them every day."

Peter and his family adjusted to life in the castle and found much to be grateful for. They all loved learning, and they were thrilled to inherit such a large library. But Peter soon became discouraged. There were so many books, but very few of them spoke of God. In addition, Peter was severely disappointed by the greed and unkindness he saw in the kingdom.

One radiant spring day, King Peter sat pondering under the huge oak tree behind the castle. He leaned his head back against the gnarled tree trunk and looked up into the canopy of leaves and the patches of blue sky showing between the branches.

My ancestor was once so kind that this kingdom was named the Kingdom of Kind, thought the king. *I feel a weight of responsibility upon my shoulders. How can I help my kingdom become kind again?*

As the birds twittered and the bees hummed around him, King Peter came up with a plan. First, he visited Eric and convinced him to write a book. This would not be any ordinary book. It was to be an autobiography of a heartless king living a self-centered life who was shipwrecked on an isolated island, found the three keys to happiness, and then learned that he was not actually a king.

Eric wrote in vibrant, beautiful, and eloquent detail about his experience of changing from a cruel, heartless, and miserable tyrant to a happy, contented, and humble orchid farmer.

This book was so popular that nearly everyone read it and felt a stirring of change in his or her heart.

Many people were encouraged to try finding the three keys to happiness themselves, and a slight change began in the kingdom.

Then the king made a huge announcement: There was to be a writing contest. All those who wanted to participate would need to write about topics that strengthened moral character and led people to follow the teachings of Jesus. The winners would have their poems, stories, or books published. Everyone wanted to read the winners' writings, and good and beautiful literature began to flood the kingdom. As more books were written about God and being generous and grateful, the people in the kingdom began following those examples. Within a few years, the citizens became happy and kindhearted, like those who originally founded the Kingdom of Kind.

And now our story circles back to where it began. It was a beautiful summer morning as Eric began a journey to the castle to visit Peter. The sunlight danced like a million shining drops of crystal along the tips of the ocean waves.

He turned a corner, and an old woman sat on the side of the path selling knitted socks. Pink pairs of socks with roses embroidered on them caught Eric's eye, and he purchased a pair for each of his daughters. As he paid the lady, he looked into her wrinkled, gentle face and gasped. It was the old woman to whom he had thrown coins that had landed in the mud.

After the old woman told him the story of the kind farmer, Drogo, who had saved her that night, Eric and the woman made a plan.

Together they traveled to Drogo's home. With glee Eric presented Drogo with seven gold coins and a silver coin— the amount Eric had once taken from the humble peasant. Eric also helped Drogo build a new cart as they talked and got to know each other.

When Drogo invited Eric to stay for dinner, a huge sigh escaped Eric's lips. An enormous weight had been lifted off of his heart.

If you could have been in that humble cottage that evening, having dinner with Eric, the old woman, Drogo, his wife Hazel, and the two children they now had, you would have heard laughter, you would have felt love, and you would have seen people who were deeply happy.

So we see that happiness does not come from being a king, or from being rich, or from having constant fun and adventure. Wherever you are, and whatever is going on around you, the three keys to happiness can always be used: gratitude, service, and work. So if you ever find yourself feeling unhappy, look around and list what you are grateful for, serve someone, and do some work, and you will soon find yourself . . . feeling happier!